Tarot Cards

&

Healing Crystals

A Beginner's Guide to Learning Tarot Card Reading & Using Healing Crystals

By
Abigail Welsh & Edson Keenan

© **Copyright 2020 - All rights reserved.**

The content contained within this book may not be reproduced, duplicated or transmitted without direct written permission from the author or the publisher.

Under no circumstances will any blame or legal responsibility be held against the publisher, or author, for any damages, reparation, or monetary loss due to the information contained within this book. Either directly or indirectly.

Legal Notice:
This book is copyright protected. This book is only for personal use. You cannot amend, distribute, sell, use, quote or paraphrase any part, or the content within this book, without the consent of the author or publisher.

Disclaimer Notice:
Please note the information contained within this document is for educational and entertainment purposes only. All effort has been executed to present accurate, up to date, and reliable, complete information. No warranties of any kind are declared or implied. Readers acknowledge that the author is not engaging in the rendering of legal, financial, medical or professional advice. The content within this book has been derived from various sources. Please consult a licensed professional before attempting any techniques outlined in this book.

By reading this document, the reader agrees that under no circumstances is the author responsible for any losses, direct or indirect, which are incurred as a result of the use of information contained within this document, including, but not limited to, — errors, omissions, or inaccuracies.

Table of Contents

TAROT FOR BEGINNERS **1**

Introduction 2
Chapter One - History of Tarot Cards 6
   The Origin of Tarot Cards 7
   Myths About Tarot Cards 16
   So, Why Do People Use Tarot Card Readings Then? 23
Chapter Two - How to Get Started **31**
   How to Pick Your First Deck of Tarot Cards 32
   Asking Questions: What to Ask and How to Do It 35
   An Introduction to Tarot Spreads 41
   Position of the Tarot Card 46
Chapter Three - Types of Tarot Cards **50**
   The Various Types of Tarot Card Decks 51
   What is Major Arcana? 59
   What is Minor Arcana? 61
Chapter Four - Meaning of Tarot Cards **65**
   The Cards of the Major Arcana: At a Glance 66
   The Cards of the Major Arcana: Meanings 68
   The Cards of the Minor Arcana: Introduction 111
   The Cards of the Minor Arcana: At a Glance 112
   The Cards of the Minor Arcana: The Meaning of Wands 113
   The Cards of the Minor Arcana: The Meaning of Cups 119
   The Cards of the Minor Arcana: The Meaning of Swords 126
   The Cards of the Minor Arcana: The Meaning of Coins 130
Chapter Five - Common Tarot Spreads **139**
   Three-Card Spreads 140
   Love Spreads 144
   Career Spreads 148
Chapter Six - Glossary **155**
Final Words **164**

CRYSTALS FOR BEGINNERS 166

INTRODUCTION 167
Chapter One - Why Use Healing Crystals? 174
Getting in Touch With Your Emotions... 175
Seek Balance... 178
Romance and Sexual Energy 179
Improve Psychic Powers 181
Improve Your Skin.. 182
Help Plants Grow... 184
Aid in Feng Shui... 185
Pain Relief... 188
Increase Your Happiness 190
Tap Into Calmness.. 193
Protection from Negative Energies 194

Chapter Two - Best Crystals to Heal Your Emotions 200
Crystals for Depression and Anxiety... 201
Crystals for Stress and Anxiety 206
Crystals for Happiness.. 214
Crystals for Love... 219
Crystals for Wealth 226
Crystals for Courage and Motivation... 235

Chapter Three - Recommended Crystals for Beginners ... 245
Hematite... 247
Citrine... 249
Blue Lace Agate.. 250
Clear Quartz... 252
Amethyst... 253
Pyrite... 255

Chapter Four - How to Use Healing Crystals 259
Meditation 260
Carrying Crystals.. 265
Drinking a Crystal Elixir 267
Bathing.. 270
Crystal Grid... 272

Taking Them to Bed *275*
Make Jewelry *277*
Block Electromagnetic Fields *279*
Decoration *281*
Chapter Five - Tips to Maximize Your Healing Crystals 289
Let the Crystals Choose You *290*
Start Slow, Add More in Time *294*
Cleanse Your Crystals Often and Thoroughly *295*
Be Willing to Experiment *300*
Final Words **304**

TAROT FOR BEGINNERS

A Practical Guide to Learning Psychic Tarot Card
Reading and Understanding the Meanings

By Abigail Welsh & Edson Keenan

INTRODUCTION

Tarot cards are a fascinating tool that people use in a multitude of ways, ranging from seeking spiritual guidance and inner wisdom all the way to simple fun and enjoyment. Unfortunately, this range of use has led to a lot of confusion around tarot. Some people consider tarot cards to be "New Age garbage" that has caught on for the same reasons as astrology and palm reading. In complete contrast are those who claim that tarot card reading involves occult powers and should never be taken lightly. Among this latter group include those who might have studied tarot card history and their use in various religious practices, but also those who don't really understand what the "powers" they are talking about even mean.

There is a path between these two approaches. That is one that respects these beliefs, whether or not they are personally believed. This middle path allows for an objective look at both sides of this belief and can look at the history, purpose, and use of tarot cards without either belittling or over-exaggerating their function. We will be following this path throughout this book. I will try to help believers and non-believers understand how tarot cards are used and why. It is my hope that this will help more people grasp this practice with sensitivity, rather than being confused by half-truths and misunderstandings.

Regardless of whether or not you believe in the occult aspect to them, tarot cards are intriguing and beautiful. Tarot card decks are primarily composed of the same cards the same way that a deck of playing cards is. But, just as you can buy many different looking playing cards, there are thousands of different designs for tarot cards that you can choose from. We'll be covering how to pick your deck in chapter two for more on this topic. Beyond the fact that they are interesting to look at, there is something very cool about watching someone use a tarot card deck properly. While there may be an occult occurrence happening in such a moment, there can be no doubt that a large aspect of any kind of reading is a psychological one in which the true desires of the self come out. This fascinating area is one of the reasons for tarot card use that we'll be exploring more in chapter one.

One of the problems with getting into tarot cards these days is the fact that there is a lot of information to learn, but also an equal number of people who seem to be spreading misinformation. If you play a game of cards or a board game with people you know, you may well have your own rules, and these are called house rules. They are representative of one group's approach to the game, but not to the game as a whole. While not a game, this seems to have happened with tarot cards to a large degree. While there is nothing wrong with following the ways your cards pull you, it isn't the same as saying, "This is how it is supposed to be done." So, acquiring a lot of good information in a sea of misinformation can be a challenge to overcome.

In this book, we'll cut through the mistruths and boil a lot of information down into an easy to understand package. In order to do this, the book will follow a simple structure that builds on the information given in a natural fashion. We'll start with the history, myths, and purpose of tarot cards in chapter one. Chapter two will teach you how to get started with advice for picking your deck and questions to ask, as well as choosing which spreads to use and exploring how the position of a card affects its meaning. From there, chapter three will look at the different types of decks and the meaning of 'major arcana" and "minor arcana." Together, chapters two and three will give you what you need to choose and use a deck. Chapter four moves into understanding the cards and the meaning of both the major and minor arcana cards. With the cards in hand, we'll use chapter five to not only learn about some of the common spreads, but we'll walk through them with easily understandable directions so you can begin using your brand new deck.

With all this information to cover, there will likely be a few words that will confuse you. You might be scratching your head already at terms like "spread" or "major arcana." While one approach to writing is to stop and explain each new term as soon as it is encountered, this would hinder the flow of the book. In order to make it easy to follow along, a glossary has been included as chapter six. While we'll be covering most of the terms naturally in each of the sections directly related to them, this glossary will provide you with a way to brush up on terms and get a jump-start on your tarot knowledge.

So, if you're ready to cut through all the confusion and get right to the heart of the cards, flip to the next page and dive into the history of tarot cards.

CHAPTER ONE

HISTORY OF TAROT CARDS

One of the most fascinating things about tarot cards is how long they have been around. They're often described as "New Age nonsense," but there is nothing new about them. In fact, tarot cards can trace their history back roughly six hundred years. That makes them centuries older than anyone who ever called them New Age!

In this chapter, we'll explore their history to see where tarot card reading came from. This will be a great way to see how the practice has developed and changed over its long history. Speaking of changing, we'll also be looking at a ton of myths about tarot cards so we can change any mistaken preconceptions we've had about them. Finally, we'll look at the meaning and purpose that people find from using tarot cards. With all this in place, you'll have a much easier time deciding if tarot cards are for you or not. If they are, then stick around because we'll start learning to pick and use them in chapter two.

The Origin of Tarot Cards

In contrast to the New Age misunderstanding, there is a similar belief that circles around them. These cards are often described as being ancient. This is simply not true. They have quite a fascinating history, but they only go back a few hundred years. This may be considered ancient to some people living today, but in technical terms, we would need to go back a couple of thousand years to reach an ancient age. There is another misunderstanding which is attached to this one. It is often reported that the use of tarot cards can be traced all the way back through this history. To a degree, this is correct; the cards were used after all. However, the way they are used has continued to alter throughout history, and so our modern version of tarot card use is nothing like their original purpose.

While the most common use of tarot cards today is divination, aka reading the future, this wasn't always the case. There is a long history of tarot cards being used for divination, but they did not start this way, and the process of performing divination through tarot has evolved and grown as well. This is reflected in the evolution of the tarot deck throughout history. If you start to look into the past of tarot cards, you will find all sorts of decks with artwork that contrasts with the expected style of tarot cards. It was only in the last two hundred years or so that the tarot card deck started to take on its modern form. Prior to this, the symbols used by the cards were often changing. There were two major factors affecting this shift. The first was time. As time caused changes in society and the world, the deck altered and evolved naturally and would often have cards that reflected issues of the time. The other element contributing to this evolution was that tarot cards became international. They started in Italy, but it wasn't long before they were all over the globe.

It is suspected that tarot cards began as cards for a Mamluk game out of Turkey. At that stage, they weren't yet in a form we would recognize. While this game was being brought into Europe, it would be the Italian lords and counts which corrupted the Mamluk game and created the earliest version of the tarot in the years before 1500. Known as *tarocchi appropriati*, this was actually a card game rather than a method of divination. Players were dealt cards at random. Each card had a figure on it, and a name, and these would be combined at random so that the player was never sure what figures they were going to get. Players would use the cards they were dealt in order to write poetry about each other. A card like the knight followed by death might end up as a tale about the tragic demise of a hero, while following it with the lovers may then suggest that love would spring out of death. The way these were laid out and displayed was referred to as *sortes*, which can be loosely translated as "destinies." This points towards their future use in divination and the use of spreads as arrangements for reading the cards.

While the poetic play of these cards had the roots of divination buried inside, the cards themselves were far from being considered mystical tools. Even while being used for *tarocchi appropriati*, these cards were primarily being used for another card game, which was more in line with those we play today like solitaire, poker, or bridge. Rich nobles had artists paint entire sets of these cards that represented kings and queens, swords and staves, coins, and wands. In time, these would see a few additions and become tarot cards as we know them today with 78 cards in a deck, which is then divided into a major and minor arcana. It is believed that these images had nothing to do with divination and everything to do with the way the game was played. Just like a royal flush is important to poker, cards like the king, death, and the fool were all important in the game that tarot cards were originally designed for. But not only that, these images were also being drawn from the world around the players. We might consider the fool and the king to be old-fashioned, but they were everyday experiences during the time of invention.

As time went on, the original purpose of the deck was essentially lost. We have records and can come up with a decent understanding of what might have been played, but for the most part, it is another chapter of history that is lost to us. Instead of the bridge-like card game, it was the *tarocchi appropriati*, which became the more widespread use. That makes sense when we consider the way these cards passed from nobility into the common population. The rules of the original game weren't spread around, but the rules of *tarocchi appropriati* were much more flexible. The order cards were played was entirely random, and it was up to the individual to divine their meaning. A shift started away from a rigidly defined system of use to one that was inspired by individuals. The lack of rules allowed for the injection of mythology and mysticism into the practice. For each person, their relationship to tarot cards might be mundane, but it might also be mystical. Every person has the ability to invest the deck with meaning and power. Although not intrinsic to the cards themselves, this nonetheless infuses them with a mystic quality, and it was this aspect that kept tarot cards being designed and created throughout for centuries after they had lost their original purpose.

The most commonly encountered tarot card deck was designed by William Rider, a publisher, and A.E. Waite, a mystic, in 1909. While this deck has been in circulation since then, never coming out of print, this was made possible by the First World War and the rise in spiritualism that came with it. As mothers and fathers were losing their sons to the war, mysticism became a subject for popular exploration by famous writers like Arthur Conan Doyle, as well as scientists like Sir Oliver Lodge and Sir William F. Barrett. The Rider-Waite deck had especially prescient timing as it came out just before the war, and it came packaged with a book that taught how the cards were to be used in divination. Waite's belief in mysticism and divination fuelled a lot of the book, but Rider's smooth thinking created a sense of unity within each suit of the deck, so there was a sense of narrative flow in the cards themselves before an individual brought their own interpretation. That made it easier for people to follow the process of divination and understand what was being drawn. But, while this created the tarot deck as we think of it, it didn't reach the levels of popularity it has today until the late 1970s.

The rights of the Rider-Waite deck eventually passed into the hands of Stuart Kaplan, a businessman who sold copper mines for a living. Not just the copper itself, but the entire mine. He was in Germany at the same time that a toy fair was going on, and so he stopped to find something for his children. It was there he first encountered tarot cards. In his language, he describes these cards as having an almost supernatural effect on him. He was compelled by them. Not only did he gain the publishing rights to release the deck, but he began to study their history and, in 1977, released a book entitled *Tarot Cards for Fun and Fortune Telling*. His efforts clearly paid off because he was able to sell more than 200,000 tarot card decks, and he has gone on to release more books on the topic. Kaplan, as well as others, has run into a bit of an issue when it comes to exploring the history of these cards. Those that use them for divination claim tarot began with mystical origins, but the historical evidence doesn't support this reading. It has led to a bit of a confusing sphere around the topic, as some see this as an insult to their belief rather than simply being the truth. Nonetheless, while the mystical aspects of the tarot deck really found their home with the Rider-Waite deck and Stuart Kaplan's advocacy of them since the late '70s, there have been a few signs which point to a deeper occult history than this story has previously revealed.

Waite was a famous mystic at the time that he worked with Rider to make the 1909 edition of tarot cards. While it would be perfectly fine to make the assumption that Waite simply took something he had seen before and added mystic qualities to it through promotion, this would be a simplification of this design process. It also overlooks an important part of A.E. Waite's life. Waite wasn't a charlatan in the way that P. T. Barnum or the Psychic Readers Network's Miss Cleo was. Waite is remembered today for two key reasons. The first is that he helped to invent the Rider-Waite tarot deck. The second is that Waite was one of the first modern historians to attempt a methodical study of Western occultism. Waite wasn't just somebody that was making things up as he went along. He was studying the origins of Western occultism as a spiritual tradition. Interested in the history of spiritualism and similar beliefs, it is likely that Waite encountered some of the more mystical uses of the tarot deck in his travels. He certainly had researched enough to be able to base the Rider-Waite deck after one of the oldest surviving tarot decks in existence. If this is the case, then Waite likely knew about some of the following mystical beliefs around the tarot deck.

Invented in the 1400s for use in a card game, by the 1700s, tarot cards were popping up more often for mystical purposes. While they had started in Italy, they had spread out over Europe by this point. Along with the spread of the cards came a spread of misinformation. Antoine Gébelin wrote about them in France, stating they were discovered in ancient Egyptian religious texts and had been brought into Europe by the wandering Romani peoples. Possibly compelling at the time, the interesting part of this argument isn't how it relates to the history of the tarot card, but what it says about interest in Egyptology at that time. Egypt was becoming a fascinating area of research and popular discussion. To many, Egypt was a place of mysticism, curses, and monsters. It was easy to believe that this strange deck of cards came from such a land. However, this would be impossible considering the fact that tarot cards had been in Europe long before the Romani people were. Not only that, but the Romani people came from Asia, and didn't have anything to do with Egypt or Africa. Regardless of this fact, this origin story was widely spread for years, and it may be responsible for a large portion of the change that tarot cards underwent at the time.

The first book on the subject would come out in 1791. Translated as Etteilla, or the Art of Reading Cards, author Jean-Baptiste Alliette discussed how he learned to divinate through a deck of 32 tarot cards and could read the future. In our world, the tarot deck is the most commonly used way to read the future through cards, but there were several other methods used throughout history. Alliette would go on to reinforce the Egyptian connection, while also making many points to differentiate it from the Egyptians to infuse his own mystic beliefs into the deck. Alliette's book would lead to a rise in interest in the supernatural qualities that had spawned dozens of books during his lifetime and thousands since.

While this history might seem to suggest there isn't any mystic quality to tarot card reading, I think that this would be an immature reading. Rather, one of the elements that sticks out in this history is the way that these cards have grown and changed organically as they have passed through history from hand to hand. What started as a simple game has managed to grow into a mystical practice. Does the fact that it was a game deduct anything from this evolution? I don't think so. Instead, I believe that we should be paying more attention to the fact that there are hundreds of different ways that objects have been used to read the future. From grains of sand to a thousand different card-based decks that have evolved over time, humanity has always used systems of controlled randomness to predict the future. I don't think it is so much the cards themselves that hold power, but, rather, it is the way in which individuals invest their own beliefs and mystic understandings into the cards. In a way, the power has been inside of us this whole time, and the tarot cards merely offer us one method through which we can tap into our inner forces.

Myths About Tarot Cards

Just as the history of the tarot card seems to be misunderstood in the popular consciousness, it is safe to say that tarot cards themselves are the subject of confusion and misunderstanding. Growing up, I heard a lot of conflicting information about tarot cards, and they prevented me from exploring the topic for several years. It wasn't even that the information I was seeking was that difficult. I only wanted to know which deck I should purchase if I were going to get one. After all, there's a massive variety of decks on the market these days. This was a simple question, but the answers I got back made it more complicated than it should be. We'll tackle these myths that I encountered first hand, as well as many that are widely shared across the internet. We'll peel back each of these myths like layers of an onion. Once we get through all of the pieces that are mistakenly shared, we will then close out the chapter by looking at the real reasons people still use tarot cards in the year 2020.

Tarot Cards Are Evil and Occult: While tarot cards date back much further, if we remember that they became most popular from 1977 onwards, then we can easily deduce where this myth came from. The "Satanic Panic" of the 1980s saw accusations that schools, churches, governments, and other institutions were dens of Satanism. Supposedly true accounts of Satanic activity led to many things being called evil. Heavy metal music, video games, early *Dungeons & Dragons*, and tarot cards were just some of the things that were posited as allowing Satanic influence over children and young people. Tarot cards are seldom considered evil nowadays, but they still get grouped with the occult. While tarot cards can be used for occult purposes, so can anything. But, in their intended use, tarot cards are simply cards. Any power they have comes from the person that is using them.

Tarot Cards are Magical: Following on from that last sentence, a simple consideration of their production should reduce any traces of the magical. You can find many different tarot card decks in bookstores. These need to be shipped, packaged, and printed en masse. This particular myth is most likely due to films and television shows which present tarot cards as having power within themselves. This same myth had my mother break my ouija board when she found it. She said she didn't want dark magic in the house. But, she allowed Monopoly by Milton Bradley, the same company that made the ouija board. Unless you have a deck that was personally made by the artist, tarot cards are mostly mass-produced. Again, it's you who brings the power. Not the cards.

You Must Buy Your Own: This is one that tripped me up when I was younger. I was looking at some tarot cards in the bookstore. A friend offered to get me some for my birthday. But I had heard someone mention you have to buy your own, so I turned my friend down and never ended up with a set from that store. There are a lot of people that spread this rumor, but it does make a lot of sense. When you buy your own cards, you browse the selection and find the set that calls to you. If you are going to invest these cards with meaning and intent, then this will make it even more powerful because there is already something there between you and the cards. While this can be a powerful connection, it doesn't make gifted tarot cards any less powerful. In fact, it might come as a surprise, but this connection is seen in many of our purchases. When we browse a bookstore in general and walk away with something we found, there is a deeper connection to that item than when we are gifted a book. We can read them both the same, but the connection to the book we bought is all ours, while the connection to the gift is a link to the gift-giver. This is a subconscious emotional investment we often make. It can help us to feel connected to our cards, but it is in no way a requirement for using tarot cards.

Tarot Cards Must Be a Gift: This is the reverse of the previous myth. In this twist, it is the connection to the gift-giver that people see as being powerful. Which connection you think is more potent or significant is up to you, but that is all this is.

You're a Psychic if You Can Read Tarot: If you are a psychic, then you are going to have a much stronger relationship to your tarot deck, and you will likely use it in a much different way than most people. But if this were true, then we would have a world with too many psychics for anyone to have missed the memo! Tarot reading isn't so much about psychic powers as it is about intuition, random chance, and perception. In a lot of ways, it is a way of asking the universe a question and receiving an answer. It might not be the answer you want, or you might not even understand it properly. But each of us has a connection to the universe since we all exist within it. This is not a psychic activity but an intimate one.

Others Shouldn't Touch Your Cards: This is one of those myths that sound more like something out of a television series than reality. The idea here is that if somebody else touches your cards, then that will drain them of your power or any power you were able to work through them. But this is not true; the power resides within you and not the cards. Of course, you probably don't want to be handing them over to your friend if he's got Dorito dust all over his fingertips, but that applies to any object we value, and has nothing to do with the power in the cards. After all, somebody had to package them and get them from the factory to the store shelf.

Cats Suck the Power Out of Cards: This is a particularly odd myth. It goes against the Western connection of cats with the occult and instead plays off the ancient Egyptians' relationships with cats. They loved their cats and had complex relationships with them, but one of the pieces of Egyptian lore that passed into the popular consciousness is that cats had the ability to send the souls of the dead to the underworld. To some degree, this got incorporated in the mythology around tarot cards, very likely due to the misguided Egyptian connection we touched upon in the history section. It should be noted that while ancient Egyptians worshipped Bastet, a cat goddess, and put people to death for harming cats, this relationship to the dead is entirely constructed by British Egyptologists. Film scholar Douglas E. Cowan discusses this at length by looking at Egyptian mummy movies and shows how this particular myth was invented.

You Need to Wrap Your Cards in…: Some people finish the sentence with silk, others finish it with wool.

Some say it needs to be leather, while others say that leather or anything that came from an animal will ruin the magic of the cards. But these cards don't have magic that needs to be brought to them by an individual. If you think they look best in leather, then wrap them in leather. Or silk or wool or anything else that either gives them a deeper meaning to you or that makes them look nicer in your opinion. Nobody else can tell you what to do with your cards, because they have a different perspective and relationship to their deck than you do with yours. Always follow your heart when dealing with tarot cards.

Tarot Cards Are Always Right: While many people that get a positive reading might wish this is true, those who get a negative reading can sigh in relief, knowing that it isn't. In a lot of ways, tarot cards are a way of asking questions of the universe. You may get back an answer, but it in no way means that the answer is correct. It might be that it is wrong from every angle, or it just might be wrong in the manner that you perceive it. More important than the answer the cards read is the answer the cards give you personally. We'll be talking about this more in just a moment. But the cards can be wrong, and they often are. This means that there is nothing in the cards that can cause you harm. A tragic reading in no way will cause you ill health or bad luck. You might experience bad luck and say that was what the reading was talking about, but this is your interpretation of the cards. They do not alter reality, but they change the way you think about your ongoing experience in a mindful manner.

The Death Card Means You Will Die: While many books and movies have insisted this to be true, it isn't the case. As dramatic as it is to pull out the death card, it doesn't mean death itself. In this sense, death is more of a metaphor. A person may get unlucky and experience a death in their family or friends after pulling a card, but this is pure chance. The card actually represents the end of something. We talk about the end of a relationship, the end of an era, the end of a work term. All of these could be described metaphorically as the death of a relationship, the death of an era, and the death of a job. These deaths are an end of one thing, but the beginning of another, and often, that new beginning is even more beautiful than imagined. So rather than worry about dying when you see the death card, you may be better off being excited about an upcoming change.

So, Why Do People Use Tarot Card Readings Then?

This is both an easy and difficult question to answer. The easiest answer is to say that there are so many reason that it would be impossible to get into them all. But this is an unsatisfying answer because it doesn't really tell us anything about this practice. The reason there are so many different practices comes down to the individual nature of using tarot cards. There are guidelines on how to use them "properly," and we'll even be looking at a couple of these before the end of this book. But, since the power of tarot cards comes from the individual using them, there is no end to the list of reasons and ways that people use these cards.

Perhaps we can narrow this down to three key reasons. These are spiritual guidance, inner wisdom, and random fate. As we look at how each one of these functions, it is useful to keep in mind your reaction to each. You might find that you entirely lean towards one reason while considering another reason to be silly. These reactions are already telling you about the relationship you have with tarot cards, and they can help to point you towards the best way to use them personally. But you might also find that you are equally drawn and repelled by elements from each of these three reasons for using tarot cards. If these categories were each separate from one another, then this might cause some confusion, but it is best to consider these reasons as three circles on a Venn diagram. They can all overlap and interchange with each other, the borders between each only as thick or thin as the individual user perceives them to be.

Let's start with spiritual guidance. In this current age, we are faced with countless decisions every day. These can range from what you should wear to where you should shop, how you should think, how you should act, what you should eat, what you should read or watch, and countless others. Unfortunately for us, humans are quite poor at dealing with too many choices, and so our current world has a habit of making us feel very overwhelmed, anxious, or spiritually lost. We'll talk about using tarot cards to live true to our nature in a moment, but spiritual guidance is necessary in those dark times where we lose sight of our nature. When we are unsure of how to proceed, of what to do next, of how we can deal with everything around us, then tarot might offer a lot to us. Asking the universe for advice and guidance can help us to find our way back onto the path we were supposed to be living. When used in this manner, the tarot deck is treated with a spiritual power, as if it was a direct link to the greater universe itself. Individuals can invest limitless power and meaning into this connection, and it can be a positive force in overcoming hardship and staying in touch with their spiritual selves.

Those that use tarot cards to access their inner wisdom share a lot of DNA with those that are after spiritual guidance. Inner wisdom already exists inside of us; that's why it's inner. But just because it is in there doesn't mean that we always have such an easy time accessing it. Have you become angry and realized that you were over-reacting yet still couldn't stop what you were doing? This is a common experience for most of us, especially when we are younger, which perfectly shows the way we can become disconnected from our inner wisdom. In the case of being angry, we could see the wisdom, but we couldn't act on it. A lot of times, we aren't even able to see our own wisdom. Sadness, work deadlines, groceries to buy, so many different obligations and emotional experiences, block our ability to perceive this wisdom. Using the tarot deck is one way we can get back in touch with this wisdom. As you do your reading, you pay attention less to what the cards are saying and more to the way you are reacting to what they say. If you can, try to notice that what they say is being made up inside of you as they are revealed. When we aren't sure of what we want, sometimes we do something like roll a dice or flip a coin to decide our path, and it is only once we see the result that we realize which direction we truly wanted to be pulled. Tarot cards are a more complicated version of this experience that can be used to tackle larger issues. In this method, the tarot cards are being used to help clear a way through everything that is blocking you from the wisdom that was in you all along.

Many of those that view the tarot deck as random fate still find plenty of joy in using it. Like a dice roll or a flipped coin, a tarot deck might simply be consulted to see what happens in a matter that isn't overly important. This view may also see tarot cards as a game, a fun distraction in line with pulling a rabbit out of a hat or getting their palm read at the local fair. Many tarot card readers consider this approach to be disrespectful, but one person's lack of belief should not invalidate another's. Tarot cards themselves are not magic in any way. The power that they hold is deeply personal, and so if someone does not feel that power, then that only speaks about their relationship to tarot cards and not tarot cards themselves. As an interesting addendum, the randomness that comes from looking at the deck without meaning finds some uses in those that are interested in Chaos magic. Randomness and uncertainty is a major theme of those beliefs, and randomly pulling from a tarot deck can take on a lot of meaning because there is no further meaning beyond the rule of chance.

That said, many in this community find that 78 cards are too restrictive to represent true chaos.

Regardless of which camp you find yourself in, neither is better or worse than another. What is important is that you approach tarot cards from your own unique, personal perspective, and you use this to guide your relationship to the cards. If you're excited to get your hands on some cards, then you're going to want to jump into chapter two right away.

TAROT FOR BEGINNERS

Chapter Summary

- Tarot cards are often thought to be a New Age invention, but they actually date back several hundred years. They began in the form of a card game that slowly morphed into a fortune-telling game.

- Tarot cards took on their modern form in the early 1900s and have continued in this manner since.

- The most common tarot deck is the Rider-Waite deck that set the mold for the modern deck.

- There are many myths surrounding tarot cards, which can make it hard for people to get started.

- Tarot cards are not evil and, while some people use them for occult purposes, they are not themselves occult objects.

- Tarot cards aren't magical, either. A person may bring their own magic to it, but this comes from the person and not the cards.

- There is a myth that you must buy your own tarot cards, but this isn't so.

- There is another myth that you have to be gifted a set of cards, and this is also false.

- Some people think that only psychics can read the tarot, but this doesn't make any sense.

- It is fine to let people touch your cards; that won't take away your power.

- Cats don't drain tarot cards of their power. The power comes from you.

- You can store your tarot cards however you like.

- Tarot cards aren't always right, and they can be easily misunderstood, too.

- Drawing the death card does not mean that you or anybody else is about to die.

- There is no right or wrong way to use the tarot deck so long as what you do feels right. However, there are some general reasons that people consult their decks: spiritual guidance, inner wisdom, and random fate.

- Some believe that the cards are a way to access higher spiritual guidance, and they use them as a way to infuse this into their lives.

- Others use the cards to discover wisdom and desires that were inside of them all along, using the cards as a way to read their true selves.

- Others use the cards as a way to speak to the universe, to invite the randomness of the cards to help guide them through life.

In the next chapter, you will learn how to pick your very first tarot card deck. If you have a deck, then you're going to want to ask it questions, so we look at how to choose questions that are right for tarot. We'll look at picking a spread and what the position of the cards mean when they are laid out. You'll have everything you need to start laying cards, but not the knowledge necessary to interpret the results. You'll need to read chapter four and the meanings of cards for that information.

CHAPTER TWO

HOW TO GET STARTED

If you're still reading, then that means tarot interests you enough to want to learn how to do it yourself. That's wonderful. With something as personal as tarot card reading, the only way to truly understand it, and get a sense for how it fits into your life, is to try it yourself. We've already talked about the many reasons why all the misinformation about tarot cards makes it hard to get started, so we can skip all of that. In this chapter, we will get straight to the point so that you can pick your first deck and start preparing yourself for your very first reading.

Don't worry; it's going to be a lot easier than people make it sound.

TAROT FOR BEGINNERS

How to Pick Your First Deck of Tarot Cards

When it comes to picking your first deck, there doesn't need to be any mysticism or magic surrounding it. If somebody has given you a deck of tarot cards as a gift, then you are going to be perfectly fine using those. That is, you will be fine using them if they are comfortable for you. Picking out a deck of tarot cards is pretty much the same as picking out anything - you want to find something that will match you. If you have big feet, then you purchase big shoes, after all! We'll look at these practical considerations, but first, let's return to the idea of connection.

As you browse for your first deck, you are going to see all sorts of different shapes and sizes, colors, and designs. You may be keeping in mind physical considerations such as the size of the cards themselves, but you should keep yourself open as you browse. A central part of picking your deck of tarot cards is to follow the energy that forms through the connections you make to the deck. If you see a deck that calls to you, that is the deck you should go with. If it is bigger or smaller than you first intended to purchase, that isn't going to matter. The fact that it called to you will make all of these considerations seem pointless. When it comes to tarot cards or other ways in which we tap into spiritual guidance or inner wisdom, it is important to follow the energy of connection whenever it shows itself.

Beyond connection, probably the biggest consideration you are going to make is the artwork and imagery on the cards. Some tarot card decks go with a minimalist design, others may inject elements of science fiction. Many are done in medieval artwork styles, which give the cards a feeling of folk roots and historical connection. The artwork on your cards doesn't affect the way that you use them. It is entirely up to you what your cards look like, but you should consider how a new design or something as extreme as a science fiction inspired design will affect the way you personally feel when using your cards. Remember, too, that if you do readings for other people, a newer style may throw them off. A lot of people think that tarot cards are ancient mystical tools and so it may lead to better readings by sticking with an old-fashion design rather than a new one. It's always helpful to consider both sides of the experience.

As already mentioned, tarot cards come in different sizes. Some can be as large as a hardcover book, while others are the size of playing cards. How large your cards are will impact upon how much space is required to use them. It will also make it harder or easier to shuffle them depending on the size of your hands. If you want to make your deck stand out from a pack of playing cards, then it can be fun to get cards that are just a slight bit larger. They'll still be quite easy to shuffle, but they will feel a little bit different when held, and this will allow you to associate this new card size with your tarot cards.

TAROT FOR BEGINNERS

This is an easy trick to make your tarot cards stand out and form a deeper bond inside your subconscious.

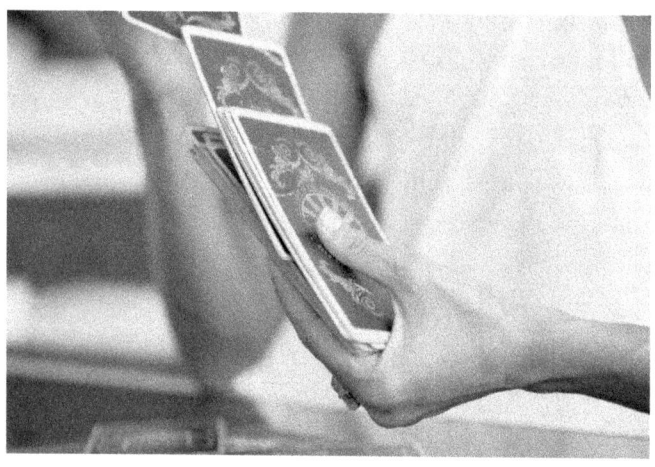

Finally, you should also consider the quality of the cards. If they are $2.99, there's probably a reason. Cheap cards will work just as well as high-quality cards do when it comes to readings, but they are going to rip, tear, crease, and stain far easier. You will likely also find that cheaper cards just don't seem to shuffle properly for some reason. Rather than each card being an entity unto itself, cheap cards like to get stuck together, and then tear when you try to separate them. This is OK if you're just purchasing some playing cards, but tarot cards require a connection, and it is hard to form a close link with a deck of cards that is constantly falling apart on you. It may cost a lot more to get a high-quality deck, but it will last much longer and cause far less frustration.

But even with all that said, remember that your connection to your deck is uniquely yours. If your first deck of tarot cards were cheap and always breaking, then maybe that is how you think of your cards, and so you only purchase cheaper decks. All those reasons that are frustrations for one person could be pluses to another. When it comes to you and your cards, follow the feeling in your gut. That feeling is more significant than any of the other concerns we've covered.

Asking Questions: What to Ask and How to Do It

The purpose of tarot cards is to reach spiritual or inner wisdom, and the only way that we can do that is through asking questions. If we didn't bring a question to the tarot reading, then we can't expect to find any answers. Asking the right question is so vital to having a successful and productive tarot reading. If you ask the wrong questions, then you are going to find yourself confused with answers that don't make sense or upset with answers that don't reflect your true intentions and desires. There aren't any rules as to whether one question is right and one question is wrong. Since what is in your heart is more important than any single rule could be, there would be no point. But there are some easy to follow steps that we can take to make sure we are asking questions that open us up to the full spectrum of the tarot instead of limiting ourselves to a disappointing experience.

What you want to learn from the tarot deck will be determined by you. There is no limit to what you can ask from it. You might meet somebody that uses theirs exclusively in matters relating to their career, another person with matters only of the heart. Your relationship to the tarot deck will be uniquely yours. So the content of the questions will almost entirely be up to you with no limitations whatsoever. Instead, the issue doesn't come from what we want to ask the tarot deck, but the way we go about doing it. We want to ask questions in a manner that is fitting of the tarot deck and the way that it performs. This means we'll want to avoid closed questions, stay within our own consciousness, focus on the now, and be proactive, and accountable to ourselves and the deck. These aspects may sound complicated, but they're easy to do, and once you start asking questions in this manner, you'll find that the deck is much more approachable and inviting.

When it comes to asking the universe questions, tarot cards have a lot of flexibility in their ability to answer. To make a comparison with a retro favorite, a magic eight ball has a total of 20 answers for the questions you ask of it. The tarot deck provides between 76,000 and 456,000, depending on how you consider the minor arcana cards. You can ask a magic eight ball a yes or no question, and you have a pretty good chance of getting back a yes or no answer. But with the tarot deck, you are going to get back much longer and much more complicated responses. With such a large range of possible answers, it is essential that we consider how open our questions are.

Closed questions have only a small number of possible responses. "Will you marry me?" is a closed question because the only answers are "yes," "no," and "I need time to think about it." "What time is it?" is a closed question because the only appropriate answer is the time or a close approximation of it. Most of the questions that we ask are closed questions, with a specific goal in mind. In contrast, open questions allow for much deeper answers. If you asked, "Will my book get purchased?" then you will get back a yes or no. If you ask the much more open version of the question, "What can I do to make sure that my book sells?" then you have opened up the range of answers. It could be to hire a marketing firm or take a class on digital promotion. You may need to research your niche in more depth to bring a perspective that is lacking from the competition. It may be to follow up on emails with that publisher you had been speaking to. The end goal of the question is the same, you want a book that sells, but the way you reach it is open. This is great for our psychology and perspectives because it makes us much more fluid and adaptable when plans change. Plus, it is great for the tarot because it allows it to answer with its full depth and flexibility. It may seem weird to ask questions this way, but once you get used to it, you'll see improvements in your readings and often even your life.

Sticking with your own consciousness is important when practicing tarot cards, regardless of your relationship to the deck. If you channel your own energies and magic through the deck in your readings, then it is inappropriate to do readings about other people without their consent. However, if you are using the tarot to tap into inner wisdom, then you might be able to understand why this won't work for you either. Any inner wisdom the deck allows you to reach has to come from inside you to begin with. You are your own person, a single consciousness. You do not have the ability to access another person's consciousness in order to speak for them and see their lived truth. This means you will never be able to properly ask a question about another and get a real answer. The answer you receive will always be in error because it will be your interpretation of a person's wants and desires rather than any truth from the universe or the cards. Even when you do a reading for another person, it will largely be the individual that interprets and makes sense of the reading you perform for them.

So, if you want to stay with your own consciousness, then your questions should reflect this. You might want to know about the way your boss is feeling, or if the apple of your eye has their heart set elsewhere.

Regardless, think not about them, but about how you relate to the situation. If you're asking about your boss because you're after a promotion, then cut to the source and ask what you can do to impress your boss. This is focused on the self, whereas, "Does my boss respect me?" is focused on the other person. Staying with yourself will allow you to keep the focus where it truly matters. You aren't asking the tarot deck questions for other people; you are asking because they have an impact on you. Make sure that you always ask from within your own conscious experience, so that you can get straight to the core of why the question is important in the first place.

Just as we must stay with ourselves, it is necessary we remain in the present as well. While we often use the tarot cards to look towards what we should do, we don't use the deck to predict the future or focus on the past. Everything that has happened has already come to pass, so the tarot can tell you nothing about them that you don't already know. Everything that is to come can be changed at a moment's notice by world events, personal events, or worse. We exist in the now, and this is where we are most able to access the wisdom of the tarot. Since we live in the now, it is our actions in the present that build the future we come to inhabit. We often forget about the present because we get so lost in the past or the future, but if we remember that the tarot deck is most powerful when approached through the present, then not only will we ask better questions, but we will find a lot more time on our hands than we knew we had. When we start living in the present, our world begins to look a lot bigger and filled with many more opportunities.

Focusing on the present is not hard. Rather than asking questions such as, "What will happen next?" or, "Was that the best action I could have taken?" you should ask questions such as, "What can I do to make sure events work in my favor?" or, "How can I treat this outcome in a positive manner?" When you start to focus your questions on the present around you, you will find that you begin to get answers which you can put into action, and that you stop trying to imagine the future, and instead, you start to build it. As you are getting ready to ask a question, stop, and consider if it is one in which you are focused on yourself in the present. When you are stopping and doing this, you will naturally be more accountable to yourself and to the deck.

Being accountable to the deck and yourself means you ask questions that are within your control and capability. If you have never once picked up a paintbrush, then a question such as, "Am I going to be a famous painter?" is going to be breaking this guideline (as well as being a closed question about the future). If you asked, "What can I do to improve my painting skills?" then you are going to have a much better result. Rather than fabricate a version of reality in which you achieve something outside of your control, you instead search for the answers that are going to provide you with the necessary advice and actions needed to live more fully. The tarot deck does not change the future, and so if you aren't being honest and accountable in your questions, then you will find that you never have an easy relationship with your deck. Dishonesty and unrealistic expectations can leave you angry and frustrated with your deck and tarot cards in general.

When you follow these basic guidelines, you will find that the questions you ask the tarot cards are much more clear and direct. Since they're open rather than closed, you will be able to get complex answers and truly tap into the deep wisdom of the cards.

An Introduction to Tarot Spreads

People might talk about different spreads as if they had some inherent meaning in and of themselves. Part of this comes from the mystique of the name. If they were just called a layout, then it wouldn't sound nearly as cool, but, in reality, that it is all that a spread is. You could use a deck of tarot cards and lay them out in any order that is relevant to you, and you would technically be using them right. You might get on the nerves of people who are very particular in their own relationship to the cards, but you are free to create spreads in any way that is meaningful to yourself. When you are using a tarot deck, you are opening yourself up to an incredibly high amount of chance. If you are asking open-ended questions, then you will have a much easier time getting answers. This can be made even more likely through the use of a spread designed for the kind of question you are asking.

Since a spread is just a layout, there are spreads for love and careers. The cards are always the same, so what is being changed with a spread is not just the placement of the cards themselves, but the symbolic meaning they've been invested with. A very simple spread is to do three cards together for past, present, and future. A simple and fun trick for those learning tarot, it isn't a particularly valuable reading since we've already left the past behind, as discussed in the last section. By changing the meaning of each card by designating it a purpose in the reading, you have much greater control over the questions you can ask. If you have ever played one of those Mad Lib word games where you pick verbs and nouns to create funny stories, then this might seem familiar. Rather than filling out a single word, a card fills out the empty slot. Tarot cards are never easy to read, and so there are a lot of ways these readings can be interpreted, and it is far more complicated than those word games, but the principle behind it is the same.

We are going to be looking at how to do a few spreads of our own in chapter five, so we're not going to cover how each spread is done here. This would slow down our conversation and turn it into a series of steps to be followed. Using a spread is very easy, and you can find many of them for free across the internet with a little bit of Googling. What is more useful for our discussion right now is how to pick the right spread. You might have questions about work, and so a career spread probably sounds right up your alley. A love spread pretty much speaks for itself. But there are plenty of questions which these spreads don't work for. Sometimes, it isn't immediately obvious what kind of spread you should be using. Picking the right spread is going to be determined by what you want to ask, how much you want to know, and what you know already.

Starting with the question, you are going to want the spread you pick to be able to give you an answer. If I have a problem, then I might do a very straightforward three-card spread. The first card represents the nature of the problem, the second card is the cause of it, and the third card would be the solution. A simple three-card spread can be used for love, work, and pretty much anything else you want to ask. Seriously, a three-card spread is the easiest thing in the world, and you can always play with and adjust each piece. Adjusting them while asking the same question over a period of time can significantly help to open up your understanding of the cards and the question at hand.

Of course, since a three-card spread is so easy to adapt to everything, it can also feel very surface level. It never really seems to go deeply into a particular problem. It can be a great way to start investigating something with the tarot deck, but often you will find that you want to go a little bit further. It isn't even that you want to get more information, so much as you want it to be more specific to the task at hand. By distilling your problem into a question for the cards, you will understand the question enough to seek out an appropriate spread. If it's about love, life, health, wealth, fertility, spirituality, healing, or more, you will be able to find many spreads that fit. By understanding the question, you can pick the spread that will give you the most desirable information.

That information should be your next determining factor in which spread to use. We've talked about this in parallel in the previous paragraph. A spread that is more specific doesn't necessarily give you more detail, but most of them will. However, there are general purpose spreads that also allow for a lot of detail. The more detailed a spread is, the more the various cards are going to be interacting and influencing each other. That means that correctly reading a more complicated spread takes time. Time to learn, but also time to perform. We'll talk about time to learn in a moment, but time to perform is important to note because a complicated spread is always, by its very nature, going to take longer to read. This isn't a problem for many people, but it is good to remember because nothing is worse than a rushed reading, and even more so, one that is cut off right in the middle. The more detailed the answer you want, the longer and more complex the spread is going to be.

Finally, it is important to keep in mind how much you know and what you are comfortable with. If you are working with three-card spreads, then it is straightforward to read each part of the spread because they interact with each other in a sequential order. But more complicated spreads have complex interactions that can be modified, facilitated, or interrupted by other cards as they are revealed. The order in which each piece is revealed, and the position the card is in, as well as its place in the spread, all alter and change the meaning of the card. That can take a lot of time to read. If you are doing a reading for a friend, then it probably isn't a good idea to reach for a complicated spread that you haven't gotten much practice with yet. It is great to push yourself to try new things, but there is a time and a place where the old and reliable comes in handy.

The cool thing about tarot cards is that while it takes a while to learn what each card means and how they interact in a spread, once you do understand, it becomes a lot easier to read. With experience, you can make complicated spreads look easy. Start with some simple three-card spreads, or some of the spreads later on in chapter five. Once you feel comfortable reading a few different three-card spreads, start practicing with a more complicated variation, and working your way up. With practice and patience, you can read even the most difficult and complex ones like an expert.

Position of the Tarot Card

The position of the tarot card is going to change depending on the spread that you are using. More than anything else, this is going to have the biggest impact on the position of the card. If you are doing a three-card spread, then you will have three cards in a row, and their meanings change depending which is first, middle, or last. What that meaning is will come entirely from the spread itself.

Many spreads are done by placing the cards out in order, but some involve laying cards in odd positions either on purpose or by random chance. You may find that some cards invoke new meaning when they are reversed ("hiding") or turned on their side ("laying down"). We'll be looking at cards in detail in chapter four, and we'll see first-hand how each of the different cards has its meaning. How laying down or hiding affects each card is mostly in the eyes of the interpreter. There is no right or wrong to these, but they mostly help the reader to get a little deeper into the core of the answer.

Note that positions in a spread are very malleable. There are spreads that are taught in many different ways. A Celtic cross spread may assign vastly different meanings to the first four cards compared to what another reader believes them to mean. So if you start to read a spread in a manner that works for you, and someone tells you it's wrong, remember they are your cards and how you read them is between you and the cards. So long as you understand the position you are placing the card into, you are still on track. If you can understand how the spread works to provide an answer, then you are using your cards exactly as you are meant to.

Chapter Summary

- There are all sorts of different shapes and sizes and designs that you can choose from for your first deck of tarot cards.

- Look for a connection with your cards and choose based on this. This connection is the most important thing you can get from a deck.

- You may also want to pick a deck that has artwork that captures your attention.

- Tarot decks can come in large or small sizes, and so you should get a size that is comfortable for you and which you can use in the space available to you.

- Get high-quality cards rather than cheap cards so that you can have a longer-lasting and better experience and relationship with your deck.

- You can ask any question you want to the tarot deck, but if you ask your questions by following certain guidelines, they are more productive.

- Ask questions that are open and allow for many answers.

- Stick with questions about yourself and how you relate to others rather than asking questions about other people.

- Stay true to the fact that your actions are your own, and you have to be responsible for them.

- Stay in the present. You can look to the future, but don't forget where you are, and that action in the now is how you get to the then.

- Tarot spreads are ways of laying cards out so that they take on different meanings. Each space in a spread has a meaning that the card then comments on.

- Cards take on different meanings when they are in different places in a spread, or if they are laying down or upside down.

In the next chapter, you will learn about the many different tarot decks and how cards differ from each other. You will also learn about the major and minor arcana to see what these mean and how this affects the cards that fill them out.

CHAPTER THREE

TYPES OF TAROT CARDS

While a traditional tarot deck comes with 78 cards, this isn't always the case. Some people prefer to use a deck with only cards from the major arcana. This will create a more compelling and interesting reading, though not necessarily any more accurate than doing a reading normally. Regardless of whether you use both arcanas, or only one, there are many different types of tarot decks which you can choose from when picking your own. These range from the classic Rider-Waite deck through to the Angel Oracle deck or the Druid Craft deck. We'll be covering the differences between each of these in this chapter.

We'll also be looking at both the major and the minor arcana so that we can get a sense of what they are. With a name like "major arcana," your first assumption is likely to be based on the similarity to "arcane." However, there isn't anything particularly supernatural about an arcana. Rather than deal with the occult, the arcanas are a way of dividing the tarot deck into two sections. We'll look at each of them carefully to close out this chapter. If you are looking for information on what each individual tarot card means, then you'll want to skip ahead to chapter four.

The Various Types of Tarot Card Decks

Since most tarot decks come with 78 cards, the choice of tarot deck should be made through your link to a particular deck. Being drawn towards the cards is crucial, as it lets you bond with your deck even before you get it open and have a chance to use it. But if you have been reading tarot cards for a while, then you've probably heard mention of a few different types of decks. A lot of people hear about them when they are first getting into tarot and are unsure of what to pick. Everyone suggests this or that kind of deck, and it quickly becomes overwhelming for a beginner. It is for this reason that we talked about choosing a deck based on how you connect to it first, rather than because it is of one particular kind or another.

Since you have your first deck now, we are safe to look into the different kinds. You may find one that draws you even more than your own deck does. If this is the case, then there is nothing wrong with you, your cards, or your desire. Many tarot users have multiple decks. Some they invest with an aura of love, only asking that deck questions of the heart. Another might be used for problems of the soul, another for issues in the career. Nothing says you need to settle for a single deck, so don't feel bad or overwhelmed if you find yourself wanting a second or even a third deck. The essential thing is you are enjoying yourself and finding meaning through your interactions with your decks. If that's the case, then you are doing great.

Each of the following decks includes 78 cards. That is 22 cards of the major arcana and 56 cards of the minor arcana, which are then divided up further into four suits that each has 14 cards. The biggest difference you will find between these decks is an aesthetic one. While the look of the cards doesn't have a direct impact on the reading in terms of which cards are drawn, they do impact the way that you interpret the cards. This impact is even greater in those you are reading for. The look and design of the cards are all a client has to go on if they don't know the meaning of the cards themselves. If you are using a bright and cheerful deck, then they are far more likely to take your reading lightly or in a positive direction. A darker, more twisted looking deck, is going to result in darker interpretations. Keep in mind that this is a subconscious effect that happens without either of you being aware of it directly. If you are only using one deck, then something neutral is a good way to go, not too cheerful, but not too dour either. This alone is a great reason to use multiple decks.

Speaking of multiple decks, there is nothing that says you need to use a single deck. You could combine cards from different decks or perform readings using two decks to answer the same question. While there are plenty of people who will see this as insulting, there are no laws against it. The only rule is what you feel in your heart and soul as you work with your cards. If you are drawn to use multiple decks together, then that's for you to follow. You might find that mixing two decks doesn't work, as different designs on the back of the cards can make it easy to tell which cards are which. However, you may take the major arcana from one deck and the minor arcana from another to create a whole new deck. You will be able to tell apart the major and minor arcanas, but not what each card is until it is drawn and revealed. A combination deck like this can easily work in many traditional spreads, though you will either need to search for or invent your spreads to use multiple decks together. Let the fact that creating new decks and new spreads is encouraged sink in. If someone is getting upset with you for how you use your tarot cards, then they're the one in the wrong because you are free to use the cards as you see fit. The connection is your own. Now, on to the decks.

We've already mentioned the Rider-Waite deck a few times throughout the book, so it makes sense to begin here. For many people, it is the cards from the Rider-Waite deck that they see in their heads when they hear somebody talk about tarot. As regards what has historically endured, the Rider-Waite deck is among the oldest of the tarot decks still in circulation. In fact, more Rider-Waite decks have been sold than any other single deck. Add the sales of the others together, and you still won't come close to the popularity of the Rider-Waite deck. Most of the decks seen in movies and television are Rider-Waite decks, and the artwork on the cards has become so famous that it graces the cover of many a rock album. The Rider-Waite deck is an excellent choice for a mostly neutral reading. Since the artwork of the deck has a medieval feeling, clients are more likely to accept Rider-Waite as a real occult tool rather than just a deck of cards. While not an occult tool, this does make the Rider-Waite a powerful device for performing readings for clients or friends.

Another famous deck is that of the Angel Oracle. The oracle deck is not actually a tarot deck in the traditional sense, so in many ways, it doesn't belong in this book. However, it is used to produce similar readings, and it is often lumped into discussions on the tarot, so we'll briefly consider it here. The Angel Oracle deck is the name for a specific kind of oracle deck. These decks are made of 36 cards that are split up into their own categories. These are form, creation, and paradise. Already, this stands in contrast with the 78 cards of the tarot, which are divided into the major arcana and the minor arcana, with the minor arcana further subdivided into four suits. Rather than the swords, cups, wands, or pentacles suits of the minor arcana, the oracle deck only uses its own three categories. With the Angel Oracle deck, the cards use images of divine angels for all the artwork. Each card also has an uplifting saying on it, so that it offers value even when you can't interpret the card itself. While these decks are often suggested as an easy way to get into tarot, they aren't actually tarot but are more like a spiritual sister. The Angel Oracle deck is particularly good for doing readings with Christians. While easier to learn, reading an oracle deck is a different skill from tarot card reading.

The Universal Marseille tarot deck is one of the more beautiful sets out there, in my humble opinion. While

Rider-Waite is more popular, the Universal Marseille deck traces its origins back much further. We saw that Arthur Waite had a lot of occult credibility when he was making the Rider-Waite deck (he was a member of the Hermetic Order of the Golden Dawn, after all), and so this led to that deck's old fashioned style. The artwork for that deck was created by Pamela Colman Smith. Smith, also known as Pixie, met Waite at a meeting of the Golden Dawn, and in 1909 they produced the deck with the help of Rider. While Waite and Pixie make for captivating biographies, they joined the party more than 150 years after the Universal Marseille deck did.

A man by the name of Claude Burdel invented this particular deck in 1751. He has been intrigued by a deck he encountered in Switzerland, and he was determined to make his own. Burdel didn't have immediate access to a printing press, so he looked around to see what he had to hand. This led to him making his deck entirely out of woodcuts. The influence of the artwork comes from the Swiss deck that he'd seen. The Universal Marseille deck is based on this woodcut deck that Burdel made in the 1700s. It has an even older style and aesthetic than the Rider-Waite deck, though there isn't the same mystical quality to the artwork. The artwork instead gives the impression of the Dark Ages, which is helped by the fact that it has very simple colors. Reds and blues are featured in abundance, with yellow for gold and trim. A little bit of green is included, but the cards are almost entirely kept in a three-color contrast. This gives them a brighter appearance than the Rider-Waite deck. That may allow for happier readers, though the deck is less likely to impress those that seek out tarot readings because they heard they were a supernatural practice.

A similar deck is the Renaissance Tarot Deck that Brian Williams designed. Williams' deck uses images inspired by the Greek gods. Each of the four minor arcana suits is represented by a particular mythological deity such as Cupid or Hercules. Where the Universal Marseille offers bright colors that stand out, the Renaissance Tarot Deck uses subdued colors that all blend into each other. You need to take a moment to really look at these cards to take in just how complicated the artwork is. This deck gives a precise tone, but the pastel colors do well for a reading in a comfortable setting, especially when asked about questions of love.

The Legacy of the Divine Tarot and the Druid Craft Tarot Deck both function under the same general idea. The Druid Craft Tarot Deck uses images inspired by Pagan ideas, so there are pregnant mothers and forest goddesses and lots of green tones. The Legacy of the Divine Tarot deck has a much more Postmodern appearance to the cards. These cards use loud colors that leap off the page, with imagery that evokes a modern-native feeling. Both of these decks are wildly popular, but their designs point towards the subculture that each is aimed at.

One of the more interesting modern decks is The Wild Unknown Tarot. Kim Krans made this one, creating the art and writing the included guidebook. While the other modern tarot decks try to look either like they came from the past or use images that directly call to the past, the Wild Unknown Tarot is the only modern tarot deck that feels like it is done with the past and ready for what awaits in the present and the future. It conveys a sense of wild, unknown territory. However, this doesn't take away from the deck's power in the least. The cards focus more on the immediate family (husband, wife, father, mother, son, brother, sister, daughter), rather than on esoteric titles such as king or queen. Perhaps that creates a more grounded feeling to the cards. Speaking of which, the illustrations that Krans uses mix strong black and white roots with loud and vibrant colors that dance off each card. They are immediately eye-catching, without relying on the intricate detail that the Legacy of the Divine Tarot or the Druid Craft Tarot Deck does. You'll find beautiful nature scenes and a wide range of animals on the cards, but there are no humans in sight. This creates a timeless feeling to these modern cards and makes it clear why it is one of the best selling tarot decks ever made.

What is Major Arcana?

The tarot deck is divided into two sections with 22 major arcana cards and 56 minor arcana cards. This can be thought of as a division between the trump cards and the rest of the cards. Remembering that tarot cards get their root in card games, we can think of them a little bit like a regular deck of cards. In a deck of playing cards, there are four suits, and each of those suits has a joker, a queen, and a king. If we were to put this into terms of major or minor arcana, then the joker, queen, and king would be the major arcana while the 1, 2, 3, 4, 5, 6, 7, 8, 9, and 10 would all be the minor arcana. This is an easy way to think of the major and minor arcana, but there is one little problem with it. It isn't that smooth.

The problem with trying to make a one-for-one comparison with a pack of playing cards is the size of the decks. There are 78 cards in a tarot deck, but only 52 in a pack of playing cards, 54 if you count the two jokers. A pack of playing cards has 13 cards in each suit, but a tarot deck has 14 cards in each minor arcana suit. That gives us the 56 minor arcana cards, and we're already at a bigger sized deck compared to our playing cards. A further problem appears when we look at minor arcana and realize that these suits each have their jack, queen, and king. So, really, a pack of playing cards is a better way to understand the minor arcana cards rather than the deck as a whole. However, the trump card metaphor still stands.

A trump card is a card or a suit of cards that has been chosen to be more valuable than the other cards. In the game of blackjack, we treat ones, jacks, queens, and kings as trump cards when compared to the other cards. The 8 in a game of crazy eights is a trump card. In tarot cards, the major arcana is composed of trump cards that are more valuable than the minor arcana. This is likely due to tarot's origins from earlier card games. The cards in the major arcana are all named figures, each of which very likely had some role to play in the original function of the game, but that has since been lost. They came to be known as major or minor arcanas in the 1800s through the writing of Jean-Baptiste Pitois. Just exactly what is this occult significance to the major and minor arcanas seems to be fluid depending on where you look. Some claim it to come from Egypt, others from Italian origin.

For the most part, the major arcana are thought of as symbols that gain their meaning and value through metaphor and allegory. There are 22 major arcana cards, though they are labeled as 0-21 rather than 1-22. Figures in the major arcana range from The Fool to The Devil, The Lovers to The Chariot, and The Empress to The World. We'll be looking at all of these in more detail in the next chapter to see how they are interpreted and understood. But first, let's take a look at the cards in the minor arcana.

What is Minor Arcana?

Continuing from our previous section, we have already learned that the minor arcana is composed of 56 cards that are divided into four suits with 14 cards each. What each of these suits is called, and how it works in a particular deck, may differ from each other, but they work pretty much the same way regardless. The Latin sees these as wands, coins, cups, and swords, while the French see them as clubs, diamonds, hearts, and spades. Elemental based interpretations assign these as fire, earth, water, and air, while a class-based interpretation settled on artisans, merchants, clergy, and nobility.

Each of these suits is broken down into the same cards. Ace, two, three, four, five, six, seven, eight, nine, ten, page, knight, queen, and king. The page, knight, queen, and king are the trump cards of their particular suit, but these are all still trumped by any of the cards in the major arcana. More than anything else, the minor arcana cards are going to pop up most often to alter or impact the reading of a major arcana card. If the major arcanas are the big players, then the minor arcana are the staff and support that make it possible. Or, another way of thinking about it, the major arcana point to the big key elements and the minor arcana allows us to get a more accurate reading and understanding of the powers at play.

This is pretty much all there is to know about the minor arcana, though it is worth noting there are many camps of tarot reading which place a greater emphasis on the power of the minor arcana. The Order of the Golden Dawn, already deeply involved in the creation of the Rider-Waite deck, actually assigns each card number a celestial body to deepen their understanding of the deck through their own belief system. How much or how little power you assign to the minor arcana is up to you. To get a better understanding of what is right for you, we will need to explore the cards in depth. We turn our attention to this task in the next chapter.

Chapter Summary

- There are many different kinds of decks which you can use, many are the traditional 78 cards, but with different approaches or with the suits of face cards renamed.

- You can use more than one deck if you want, there is no reason why you can't.

- The most popular deck of all time is the Rider-Waite deck, which has a very traditional style to it.

- The Angel Oracle deck is extremely popular, but it isn't a tarot card deck; it is an oracle deck, which is an entirely different thing.

- The Universal Marseille tarot deck is based on old woodcuts.

- The Legacy of the Divine Tarot and Druid Craft Tarot Deck are two examples of modern-day decks that have a very New Age feeling to them.

- One of the more popular decks is The Wild Unknown Tarot, which uses rainbow colors and a focus on scenery that makes it feel both fresh and ageless.

- The major arcana is 22 cards that make up the fool's journey. These are face cards which each represent aspects of the self and of experience which we need to take into ourselves and learn from.

- The minor arcana is made up of 56 cards. These are then broken down into four different suits, each of which has 14 different cards.

In the next chapter, you will learn what each and every one of the 78 tarot cards that make up the major and minor arcana means so that, with a little bit of practice, you can read them like a pro.

CHAPTER FOUR

MEANING OF TAROT CARDS

At this point, you have learned the history of the tarot deck and seen the many different reasons that people use them. Having chosen your own, we've gone over what questions to ask, how to pick a spread, and how the meaning of a card changes depending on where it is located. All of this provides the basic training necessary to create the foundation of your new skill in reading tarot cards. But it is time for the hardest part.

There are 78 different cards in the tarot deck, and each of them has a meaning. These meanings take on whole new depth, depending on where they are placed in a spread. To fully understand and read a particular spread, you are going to need to understand what each of the cards does. Getting the cards down so that you know them by heart is difficult, but it is necessary that you do so prior to reading for others. Without knowledge of what they mean, you can't understand how they change and differ depending on their placement. To fully understand this, you need to understand both the spread you are working with and the cards that you have in your hand. We'll look at spreads in the next chapter; for now, we've got cards to explore.

This chapter is going to be jam-packed with information about all of these cards. There's 78 of them, after all. To make it a little easier to follow, we'll start by looking at the major arcana and then move onto the minor arcana. The cards in the minor arcana all alter and affect those in the major arcana, but it is the major arcana, which is the most complicated and important. Practice with your deck at home as you read along, quiz yourself on what each of them means by shuffling the major arcana cards and drawing them randomly. Take your best guess, then double-check the answer below. These will all be old friends in no time.

The Cards of the Major Arcana: At a Glance

0) The Fool
1) The Magician
2) The High Priestess
3) The Empress
4) The Emperor
5) The Hierophant
6) The Lovers

7) The Chariot
8) Justice
9) The Hermit
10) Wheel of Fortune
11) Strength
12) The Hanged Man
13) Death
14) Temperance
15) The Devil
16) The Tower
17) The Star
18) The Moon
19) The Sun
20) Judgment
21) The World

The Cards of the Major Arcana: Meanings

0 - The Fool: The fool starts the deck, and in a lot of ways, this is reflective of the card reader. If you have ever heard of "the fool's journey," then you may know that the tarot deck is often considered to be this card's stroll through life. The fool is number zero, and so he is outside of the tarot deck, numerically, the same way that the reader is. The fool is thought to be vulnerable, as they have yet to encounter just how tough life is. But since they have not yet been tested by life, there is the opportunity for them to show great strength to rise above the hardships. But the fool can also be overwhelmed. Some seem to think, based on the name, that the fool represents stupidity or mistakes in some way. The fool is not a moron; he merely lacks life experience. When the fool is pulled, you want to align with him to take on the challenges of life with the fool's open eagerness.

1 - The Magician: The magician isn't an outside force that one encounters. For example, as the fool, you don't then meet the magician. The magician is something that is inside the reader or the person receiving the tarot reading. The magician card is meant to remind us that we are all magical in our own way. This may actually be the case with someone with magical talent, but it is also a metaphoric reading. For example, a talented musician has magic in the form of the skills they have honed over a lifetime at their craft. The magician reminds us that we are powerful but also unique, that the powers we hold are ours and ours alone. If the magician is revealed then you should take action, he reminds us that the time to act is now because we have the skills to get the job done, or the ability to learn them if we set ourselves to it. This doesn't mean that you should rush every time you see the magician. Sometimes it can be a reminder of the skills you have, a reminder to look for a better solution to your problem that is more in tune to your frequencies rather than what you're trying currently. Whether the magician is telling you to rush or wait will depend on the question and your interpretation.

2 - The High Priestess: The high priestess represents your consciousness, both the part you are aware of and the subconscious part that happens without your knowledge. Like the magician, the high priestess tells us to look inside of ourselves for the answer. The magician points us towards our skills, but the high priestess guides us towards what we feel in our guts. The high priestess is a reminder that our instincts are to be trusted, and that we have gained these innate feelings and instincts for a reason. When she shows herself in a reading, she tells us to look here, to this source of knowledge inside of ourselves, for the answer. But, just because the knowledge is inside of us, that doesn't mean it is always easy. Sometimes the knowledge that the priestess tells us to seek is that which makes us feel the most vulnerable or scared. The high priestess does not represent good or bad, but rather points us towards where we should be looking for our answers.

3 - The Empress: The empress is also sometimes thought of as the mother due to her deep-rooted ties to mother nature. But the empress is not mother nature;

she is simply linked to mother nature through her connection to beauty and love. The empress sees mother nature as something to love, as much as she loves those around her and her own existence. The empress is feminine, through and through, and this can be a reminder for us to get back in touch with that feminine part of ourselves. This applies to men as much as women. Her connection to mother nature reminds us to stop and smell the roses. She can be a sign that we have fallen out of touch with the world around us or the love we have inside. She is also a reminder that true beauty and happiness don't need to come from wealth, but from love and empathy. She is said to be a very potent card, and her presence can completely change the way you approach your question in the future.

4 - **The Emperor:** An emperor has to be a man of power, a man of force. An emperor has to be able to rally troops to his cause and keep men working under him honestly so that the needs of the empire are thought

of above the selfishness of men. So it makes perfect sense that the emperor card represents our own leadership and power. But if you aren't naturally a leader of men, then you might not think that you have any leadership skills. You'd be wrong. The emperor card reminds us that we are the emperor of our own lives, and our choices are what lead us through life. If we keep making poor decisions, then we aren't demonstrating ourselves to be very capable emperors. But when we take control of our lives and remember this part of ourselves, we can step into the present and keep our empire healthy, safe, and secure. When we become aware of our strength, we not only become aware of how we are using it but also the effect it has on others. This brings our awareness to the fact that our actions don't happen in a vacuum, but affect those around us. Poor decisions can lead to the people around us hurting, yet, with a little bit of leadership, we can bring positivity to the situation.

5 - The Hierophant: The hierophant card represents our connection to our spirituality. The hierophant is a card that represents a connection to the divine. That doesn't mean that the card itself has a connection, but rather, it reminds us to take a step back from our problem, our question, and think about it from our unique spiritual perspective. There are many problems we encounter, which cause us to get lost in the world of logic or details. We lose sight of how we feel about the problem on a spiritual level. Sometimes, we need to do what we feel and leave a project behind or remove a harmful influence from our lives. Sometimes we need to stop thinking about how we can profit, and start thinking about how we can help one another. Whatever the question is, the hierophant reminds us that answers can be found in that intangible and personal spiritual realm that is inside each one of us.

6 - The Lovers: The lovers is a favorite card of lots of people. Artwork for the lovers has been featured in many shows, movies, video games, and album covers. It is probably the third most recognizable card after death and the fool. The lovers is accurately titled, as its purpose is to bring out awareness back to our love life. Perhaps we have gotten a little bit lost in a particular problem and didn't even realize that our love life was suffering. Or maybe we've been stagnant so long, and this is a sign of something on the imminent horizon. While the lovers is most often represented in this fashion, we should keep in mind the metaphoric value of the tarot deck. The lovers can also be seen as simply a representation of something you love. The particular question you asked will make the lovers' role more apparent. If you are consulting with the tarot deck because you are unsure of where you want to go in life, the lovers are a little more ominous. They remind us to consider our choice carefully because our actions have consequences on those we love, and we may not have identified all of the possible issues yet.

7 - The Chariot: The chariot represents that engine inside each of us. We all have an inner drive that pushes us to work harder at what we love. It's why we push ourselves in the gym or on the sports field. It's why a writer tries to squeeze a page in during their coffee break, or why a doctor keeps up with the latest medical discoveries. We all have a drive inside of us, and the chariot card reminds us not to forget about this. The stress of life can weigh us down and make us lose sight of our drive. Sometimes we are distracted by too much work, and that drive starts to fade away. The chariot card reminds us that stoking that fire is the only way to keep the engine going, but that once it is working, there is no stopping where you can get to. The chariot is a formidable card that suggests great things are on the horizon so long as you grit your teeth and keep the fire burning.

8 - Justice: Depending on which deck you are using, #8 and #11 may have their places swapped. We step outside of ourselves when we consider justice. This is not a card that tells us to look inside of us or to consider personal knowledge. Instead, justice is the hard truth of the world.

It is a law that none of us can escape. When the justice card comes up, we're not talking about the kind of justice the police represent. The justice card is about karma, that universal justice that might not always be visible. It's that justice that sees bad men punished for their Faustian deals and good men venerated. Justice can be read as a harsh reminder that your circumstances are the result of your deeds. Your actions are the reason for your problems. Of course, this also means that anything positive you are experiencing is also because of your own doing. Justice is impartial when it comes to your reasons or your experience; it is just a force in the universe. However, if justice comes up, then you should take it as a reminder to be on your best behavior and not to hurt those around you.

9 - The Hermit: The hermit is another reminder that the answers we are looking for are already inside of us. That is, if the hermit comes up alone as the source of the answer, then we know that we have to look inside of us. The hermit also modifies other cards. For example, the emperor points us towards the power that we are bringing, and this isn't necessarily inside of us as much as it is something we control and use at all times. The hermit doesn't steer us away from the emperor, but he gives us a sign of the best tool to use to get at the knowledge. The hermit likes to spend time alone, his quiet, his peace. He wants to be away from people, away from noise, away from distraction. The hermit card tells us to reflect on the problem that we are facing. With the emperor card, this might mean that we should meditate and consider the way that we are using our power and whether it is helping or hurting our cause. Sometimes we get so lost in everything that we don't realize we've been surrounding ourselves with outside influence and forgotten to listen to our inner voices. The hermit is a sign that it is time for us to return to ourselves.

10 - Wheel of Fortune: No, this card isn't a sign that you're about to be a contestant on your favorite game show. Instead of the bright lights of the spinning wheel from TV, the wheel of fortune card is better thought of as a clock that we are all hanging from. We're stuck on the hands of the clock as they spin around endlessly. This is a good reminder that time takes all things from us, that the natural state of existence is change. However, the wheel is not the wheel of time, but the wheel of fortune, and this implies another truth for us to grasp. When it comes to our good fortune, it comes and it goes. Sometimes we have it, and we're on top of the world; other times, it is nowhere to be seen, and we feel like we're hanging on for dear life. The wheel of fortune reminds us that we will lose everything that we have or ever gain. There is no permanence. Some find this horribly depressing, but it is meant as a reminder to cherish the good while it is here but to be ready to accept when it is gone rather than mourn. In a spread, it reminds us that the good is temporary, but the bad is transient as well. It may be a sign that change is coming soon, or that you need to take a moment to enjoy the present. Regardless of whether it comes up in a spread or not, the wheel of fortune will continue to turn.

11 - Strength: Depending on which deck you are using, #8 and #11 may have their places swapped. The strength card isn't about how well you do at the test-your-strength game at the carnival; it's about how well you do going through the haunted house. This card is about your courage in the face of hurt and danger, and your ability to weather the struggles that life throws at all of us. No matter how low or useless or powerless you have felt, if you are reading this book, then you are still alive, and that means that you have strength inside you that you continue to tap into every day. When you feel the lowest is when you use the most strength. Depression and anxiety can be massive burdens, but if you're facing life with them and continuing to get out of bed each day, then you are demonstrating massive amounts of strength. This card reminds you of this, this forgotten strength, so that you can remember just how powerful you are. It reminds us that we have faced troubles, problems, and crises in our lives, and so this current one is fully within our capabilities to master.

12 - The Hanged Man: The hanged man is a confused character. He's often depicted as not only hanging but hanging upside down. Sometimes when you draw him, you will instinctively place him upside down because he looks like he should be standing normally. This confusing quality is wonderfully fitting as the hanged man is a sign that you are confused. You are in a liminal space between where you're coming from, and where you want to go, but you aren't sure exactly what to do. When you're confused like this, you are left feeling like you are hanging. You need to find the nail that has you trapped so that you can get out. This could be an old way of thinking, a bad habit, your credit card debt, or a thousand other things. Something has you caught up, and you need to let it go so that you can turn the world right-side up and find where you are supposed to be going again. Remember that the hanged man often has to give up something to get out. He's hanging by a nail through his clothes, so they're likely to get ripped. Getting hung up on something often results in us having to give that thing up. It might be comfortable to keep texting an ex-partner, but if you're still hung up in the past, then you can't move forward. The things we give up might be enjoyable, but if they're getting in your way, then you can't move on with them weighing you down.

13 - Death: Death is the most widely known card. As we talked about in chapter one, drawing the death card does not mean that you are going to die. Reading tarot cards is reading the intentions and meaning of the cards and how they interact with each other. If the death card comes up, then its interpretation is going to be determined by which slot it came up in. Movies like to have it come up in the future slot so that characters get a nice scare before the real action of the story starts. In reality, this would be more likely to tell you that one phase of your life is about to end, and another is about to commence. The death card is about the end of things like behaviors, influences, relationships, careers, projects, problems. The death of something good means the end of its influence in your life. This is a sad thing, but where one thing ends, something new can begin, and this can be a source of the most wonderful joy. The death card could also be thought of as the "change" card because that is what it ultimately signals.

14 - Temperance: The temperance card is like the hermit in that it is not about an answer inside of us, but about how we should go about getting to the answer. The hermit tells us that we need to seek our solitude to mull it over in silence. Temperance, on the other hand, reminds us that we need to be patient without getting upset. The temperance card finds a lot of parallels in the values of Buddhism, as it tells us we need to allow ourselves to accept that life happens in a manner that we cannot predict. Things come and things go, things change. We make plans, and then suddenly, something comes up. All of these can be frustrating, but we can choose to accept them and let them go, or we can choose to get upset. The temperance card is a reminder that this is the natural state of existence, and there is no reason to get upset about it. Instead, remember to go with the flow. Do your best, but don't get upset when things alter. Change is the natural state of all things, and life is wildly unpredictable. If you see temperance, remember this and consider how you can loosen your hold on any certainties you still have about the future.

15 - The Devil: The devil card is almost certainly the reason that some people still call tarot cards, "the devil's picture book," but it isn't about demons or the devil in a Biblical sense. Again, we're working with metaphors here. There are a lot of times in life when we feel powerless as if life is out of our control, and there is nothing we can do about it. It is in times like these that the devil is likely to appear. The devil is not only drawn by these feelings; he's the cause of them. The devil card represents the ways that we trick ourselves into thinking we are powerless. We do this all the time. In neuroscience terms, we continually reinforce negative thoughts, which create lasting impacts on the physical structure of the brain through neuroplasticity. The devil card represents these and reminds us of them. It means we have become trapped. We've forgotten that we are the source of our power and that everything inside us is under our control. The devil obscures us from seeing that we are emperors and tricks us into sabotaging our own lives. When the devil comes up, take it as a sign that there is a negative influence blocking your full potential. Look for the way to remove the devil's influence so that you can reconnect with your inner emperor and regain authority over your life.

16 - The Tower: While Christians are most disturbed by the devil card, and people fed on movies and television are scared of the death card, tarot readers hope to avoid the tower more than any other card. The tower is destruction, and it is often depicted as a burning wreck of a building. The problem with the tower is that when it comes up, we will naturally want to avoid it. That is especially true if we are doing a reading for somebody else. Nobody wants to hear about this, and others aren't educated enough in tarot to realize that it is already too late. When the tower comes up, there is only one thing left to do. It simply burns. You can't save it; you can only wait for the flames to go out so you can start to build something new. Like the devil card, the tower card comes up most often when there are feelings of hopelessness. Crumbling marriages and careers bring the tower card out to play in a hurry. It represents a painful experience, but it leaves behind fertile soil for the future's growth.

17 - The Star: The star is the polar opposite of the tower. Rather than destruction and pain, the star is a sign that healing is on the way. The star reminds us not to give up hope, and that good things are coming. Health, happiness, and good times. For artists, it means a muse is coming. For depression, it means that help is on the way if you look for it. If the tower is about the possibility of fertile soil, then the star is about planting new roots in that soil and beginning a new future. While there is no direct good luck charm in the tarot deck, the star is the closest version of it because it suggests the brightness of a new day. This is especially welcome after a long storm or the time spent burning the tower.

18 - The Moon: The moon card is one that can change its meaning greatly depending on where it is placed. In general, the moon is your subconscious, kind of like the high priestess. But where the high priestess is about consciousness itself, the moon is more about the contents of the subconscious. This means every thought you didn't realize you had and every feeling you haven't addressed is a part of the moon card. Every doubt you've never vocalized, and every fear that has driven or crippled you, all of these falls under the moon card as well. With such a wide range of areas which the moon card could represent, the spread itself is going to be important to determine which is the most appropriate. When it is pulled, the moon is often a sign that the contents of your subconscious are out of alignment. This may be the cause of anxiety and worry. We have a problem in which our subconscious takes on a lot more information than we realize, mostly due to how much time we spend watching TV or scrolling through social media. These things aren't necessarily bad in any way, but the moon card tells us that it might be time to look at the contents of the subconscious to let go of a lot of it. Fears, anxieties, stressors, misguided beliefs, anything that you didn't realize was weighing you down can be let go.

19 - The Sun: The sun is like the star in that is another card that is wonderful to see in a reading. The star offered hope because new things were coming soon, the sun informs us that we are moving in the right direction and that we should continue doing what we are doing because it will shortly be paying off for us. The sun also suggests to us that there is a lot of happiness around us, as happiness and success seem to come hand in hand. Where there is happiness, success catches up; success doesn't bring happiness, but it likes to follow behind. The sun tells us there is happiness around us and that we should appreciate what is happening and the people we know. Often, when we do this, we find that it is these same people that we appreciate that bring us the best opportunities and chances to grow. Remember that when the sun shines, things are bright, and you are making progress along the right path.

20 - Judgment: The judgment card is a call to stop and stare long and hard at your life and how it has been going. When it comes up in a reading, this card reminds us that we are working towards a future and what the future is can change at any moment. If you want to work in movies but ended up in TV because you thought it was your way in, it is more than okay to change your goal to something related to this new circumstance. You can aim for whatever kind of future you want; it is entirely up to you at any moment. You are the emperor of your own life, you get to decide. Because of this, you also know that you can change and leave your past self behind. That doesn't need to continue existing and holding you down. These are powerful reminders that will help greatly. When you see the judgment card, you should take some time to reflect on where you have come from and where you are now. Then consider where you want to be. How far have you come, and what do you need to do to get there? Is it still something you want, or is it time to set a new future? All of these are under your control, and the judgment card reminds us to recalibrate these values so we can get a better understanding of who we are and live more fully in line with our values.

21 - The World: The world represents everything, and this means the end of the fool's journey; every desire has been achieved. Each part of the tarot deck so far has either been about a part of you or the way that events are going to play out. The world represents you as each of these parts combined into a single whole. You are every other card and the lessons they hold, now in a single card. When the world is drawn, you know that you are doing well and that the road you are walking is leading you directly to your unique destiny as a complete individual. However, as wonderful as this is, it needs to be remembered that this is referring to the question being asked of the tarot cards and not just life as a whole. So, the world points towards the answer, the positive outcome, the resolution of an issue. Whether it ends poorly or well, it ended the way it needed to end for you to continue on the path you are on. The world is a treasured card because it comes at the end of the deck. The deck doesn't end on a downer. Life is an extraordinary thing according to the fool's journey, and there are hard lessons to be learned, but they're what gives us greater power over our lives, and this is a truly excellent way to end the major arcana.

The Cards of the Minor Arcana: Introduction

There are 56 cards in minor arcana, which means that there is a lot to cover. Thankfully, it is divided into four suits, and each suit is made up of the same cards. It's like a suit from a deck of playing cards, only there is one more card between the 10 and the jack. We'll take a quick glance at how this looks and then go through each of the suits individually.

The Cards of the Minor Arcana: At a Glance

Suits
Wands
Cups
Swords
Coin

Cards
Ace
Two
Three
Four
Five
Six
Seven
Eight
Nine
Ten
Page
Knight
Queen
King

TAROT FOR BEGINNERS

The Cards of the Minor Arcana: The Meaning of Wands

Wands: Wands have connections to clubs, fire, and artisans, but in their use relating purely to the tarot, they are more in line with creativity and engineering. Clever business ideas and new creative projects are all the tone of wands. But, rather than getting an idea and letting it go, wands are about action and taking risks in the name of dreams and ambitions. Wands are all about thinking of something new and then going out and doing it because without action, there is no reaction, and ideas don't have any power on their own. If you get a wand in a reading, then you need to be putting something into action soon.

Ace: The ace of wands is the first card in this suit, and so it represents the beginning of a journey, its creative and innovative aspects. The ace of wands is the first step of the new project, the idea percolating in the brain or being shared with friends. When you see the ace, keep an eye out for the project that needs to begin.

Two: Fittingly, two of wands is that second step where you go from talking and start doing. It's where you learn new ideas and test them out rather than sit at home and dream about them. When you see the two, you know it is time to run in this new direction with everything you've got.

Three: This is that feeling of joy and hope you get when you are just starting a new project. Creatives like writers love this part of a new project because it is the most exciting time, and the ideas are fresh. This reminds us that the best ideas and chances come when we open ourselves up to our creativity. If we aren't prepared to act on new endeavors, then we lose this hope, but we can always regain it.

Four: The four of wands reminds us that solid plans require reliable builders and that this often comes in the form of other people. We frequently may try to do everything ourselves, especially in the competitiveness of today's modern job market. But oftentimes, the most powerful and influential forces come from groups of people rather than any one person acting alone. Look towards the people around you that you can count on when you see this one.

Five: The five of wands shows up when there is stiff competition. This might be because you are planning to make big moves or because you have a strong opponent in your way. It is important to remember that winning is one thing, but being mean will only cause harm to those around you. The five of wands tells us to slow down for a moment, to consider who might get hurt as a result of this competition, and to consider if that is worth it.

Six: The six of wands is all about what we are getting back for our hard work. If we keep going and doing our best and continually pushing forward, we will be celebrated and respected for what we have achieved. Getting a six of wands does not mean that you are ready to stop, but rather that you are going in the right direction, and people are recognizing how much you are doing. Drawing this card reminds us to be pleased with what we've done and to accept praise with an open heart.

Seven: This card represents a happy person, content with their work. This can be a tremendous indication that we are on the right path, but this card, in particular, warns us about not getting too comfortable where we are. Change is the state of existence, and we need to be aware of where we are and ready to react to changing circumstances as they arise. Drawing a seven of wands isn't a sign that you should stop being happy but simply that you must keep working if you want everything to continue working out.

Eight: Drawing the eight of wands reminds us that everything can happen in a moment's notice. Things go fast in the real world, and sometimes we can't keep up with all the changes. But change is the natural state of things, and so we must do our best, and find new ways through them.

Nine: No matter how hard a worker you are, you are going to need to rest sometimes. If you are like me, then you're a workaholic who doesn't sleep nearly enough, so remember to take notice whenever you draw the nine of wands. This card tells us that we need to rest, to heal either physically, mentally, or emotionally. We might be working ourselves to the bone looking for a solution to a problem, and we forget to sleep. Our productivity levels are down, and we're only further away from an answer than we would be otherwise. Take time to rest when you see the nine of wands.

Ten: The ten of wands is the opposite of the nine. The nine tells us we need to rest; the ten tells us there is no time to rest! Sometimes we get into situations where the only way out of them is to keep going as hard as we can.

When this is the case, you're likely to find the ten of wands popping up in your readings.

Page: This is a very interesting card. The page is an innovative fellow who doesn't care what other people think about him. In the case of the page of wands, he wants to be free to create and carry out any weird project that comes to mind. The page's goal is a liberation of the self into pure creative investigation. That takes a lot of love and passion and desire, and it can become the source of tremendous power. We all have a page inside, but we have a hard time getting to them. When you see the page of wands in your readings, dig deep and look for that ray of light that catches your interest and brings a new meaning to your reality.

Knight: The knight of wands has a big problem. He is quick to attack the people around him rather than wait to learn their intentions. He acts fast, but that action is never well thought out. The knight acts without fear; he goes after what he wants and has no concern for what happens because of it. Drawing a knight of wands doesn't necessarily mean this is bad, but it might be a warning that you need to rein in that side of yourself so that you can get back in touch with your intelligence to plan appropriately.

Queen: The queen of wands is a formidable card. The queen acts, rather than talks or dreams. She is full of energy that leaks out to those around her and feeds them. When she brings her positive energy, this has an invigorating effect. The queen of wands is a kind-hearted character, but one that demands actions. This means that she represents a struggle to be engaged in, but she does so as a motivator. When you draw her, be proud of how you act and respect yourself when interacting with the people around you.

King: The king of wands is not just a leader, but a hero. He is a CEO, a film director, the head of a company, or the manager of any number of teams. The king of wands went out, and he made something of himself. But he doesn't stop there. The king of wands can't stop, adventure calls his name, and the only thing he knows for sure is that there is more he wants to see. He likes his position, it brings him lots of joy, and if he is wise, then he shares that joy with those around him. When you draw the king of wands, take a moment to revel in your power and how important you are. Then, once you appreciate yourself, you can turn it outwards to continue being a true hero.

The Cards of the Minor Arcana: The Meaning of Cups

Cups: In tarot, the suit of cups is most closely connected to the spirit inside each of us. This spirit is created in our connections to ourselves and our emotions, as well as to the feelings and lives of the people around us. Cups point us towards matters of the heart and soul, sometimes even the ethereal realm of dreams. These cards are connected to water and warm weather, like a beach in the summer. They invite you to dive into the water to cool off from the hot rays of the sun. They're also there for those dark nights when you want to walk alongside the shoreline and consider what you feel to be true in your heart.

Ace: We get tight and worried and lost in our fears and emotions. The ace of cups is aware of this and understands that we need a healing balm from time to time. When you draw the ace of cups, take a moment to drink from its healing waters by spending time with those you love and sharing interests and emotions freely with one another.

Two: Everyone wants the two to come up in love spreads because it represents soul mates. Of course, it doesn't need to be a romantic partner; it can be a mentor or teacher or even a good friend or a business partner. Anyone that you meld with in a strong way can fit with this cup. When you draw it, invest more time and attention into that relationship so that it remains fruitful.

Three: While the two of cups is about tight bonds with partners, the three of cups reminds us to take time to invest in our relationships with those around us who help us in our work and lives. Babysitters, co-workers, friends, family, grocery store employees, and baristas are just some of the many people that you might consider honoring. Reach out to these people and let them know that you understand how they are helping you, and you appreciate it.

Four: The four of cups is about getting stuck. You don't know where you are anymore or what you are supposed to be doing, and you just feel plain old stuck with nowhere to go. When you feel like this, you can get lost in anxiety and negativity and miss the way out that's right in front of you. This card is a warning not to get lost in our negativity.

Five: The five of cups represents a period of emotional struggle and pain. It is a time in which you are overwhelmed with sadness, or you are lost in regrets over something that you've done in the past. Maybe you didn't get a promotion, or you regret breaking up with your boyfriend. Whatever the case, we all go through these periods. The five of cups is a sign that we need to forgive ourselves and let go of the past. We must focus on the future.

Six: There is a lot of wonder and amazement in the world when seen through the eyes of a child. Everything holds such hope and promise, and there are endless possibilities. Then, as we get older, we seem to lose touch with this wonder and these possibilities. We close ourselves up to all the beauty and mini-miracles that happen around us every day. The six of cups is a sign that we need to get back in touch with this freshness and look at the world with new eyes.

Seven: The seven of cups represents the imagination. This might be an imagination with lots of wonderment, as discussed with the six of cups, but it could be a boring place if you haven't used it very much. Whatever it is, your imagination is yours to control, and with it, you can pick what your future is going to be. You can also choose what to make of the present moment, free to change your mind or stay in character. Drawing the seven of cups can let us know that we haven't enough imagination in our lives and we need more. It can also warn us when we've become lost in that imagination, and we've stopped seeing the real picture. Either way, we either have too little or too much when this card comes up.

Eight: The eight of cups is an unfortunate card to draw because it represents disappointment. Since we're talking about cups and they deal in that emotional space, this is often something like a broken heart, a mistrustful friend, or a disappointing experience. The eight of cups often appears near the end of a problem, when there is little left you can do, but accept there is pain you must deal with. When things don't work out, and you feel let down, the eight of cups comes to remind us that it is okay to be upset, but we can take that energy and put it elsewhere so that we stay productive rather than destructive.

Nine: The opposite of the eight of cups, the nine of cups shows up when things are working out, or soon will do. It is one of those cards that everybody wants in their reading because it is considered to bring good luck. When you see it, there is nothing that you need to do.

Just continue focusing on the good side of life and working hard at what you love without hurting others. It is all about to pay off now.

Ten: Another card that everyone likes to get, the ten of cups is a sign that it's time to celebrate and take stock of those you love. The ten of cups means that everywhere you look, there is love looking back at you. You have put out so much love that it now greets you wherever you go, and you have nothing to worry about. When you see the ten of cups, you can rest easy knowing that you are making tremendous progress through life and that the people around you want nothing but the best for you.

Page: The page of cups is a fascinating card. They are emotionally vulnerable and could easily be hurt if they aren't careful. They believe strongly in their ideals, and they have powerful imaginations. This can help them to seek considerable success in life and much happiness in their spirits, but they are also open to deep pain if they don't respond to the world properly. The page of cups needs to learn to protect themselves without losing touch with the youthful spirit that drives them. If you draw the page of cups, you should remember to be more like the page and open yourself up. Take risks like a child, and be ready to learn to protect yourself without losing yourself.

Knight: The knight of cups is a hero that everyone can love. He is wise and knows much about love while also being deeply intelligent about many subjects. People find the knight of cups to be charming, and he creates a seductive air without even trying. But he does this because more than anything, he is a man of action. When the knight of cups dreams up an adventure, he immediately sets forth on it. He gets beat up and takes his share of tumbles, but he always finds his way to glory in the end. If you draw the knight of cups, then take comfort knowing that you are on a brave and exciting path, and the struggles you face will end with much to take pride in.

Queen: The queen of cups is another card that is representative of our inner female and the connection we have to our emotions. The queen of cups represents love and understanding, given freely to the whole of existence rather than conditioned and given only to those that please her the most. She feels deeply and understands that emotions are fleeting experiences to be treasured, whether they be good or bad. If you draw the queen of cups, then you need to take some time and get back in touch with those feelings deep inside. Remember, too, to act like the queen of cups does, and open your heart to the world around you and from a place of love rather than negativity or spitefulness.

King: The king of cups is an impressive card. So much so that the king sits and never speaks, he radiates his authority and control. People know not to mess with the king of cups because his power is a deep one, one that

TAROT FOR BEGINNERS

doesn't require him to be flashy or show it off. It is a force to be afraid of, but not a force that he uses for fear. The king of cups has risen above being controlled by his emotions, and he doesn't use emotions to control others. He understands that feelings tell him more about himself and what he knows to be right, and this space between feeling and acting gives him great power. When you draw the king of cups, look deep inside yourself. Look at the scariest of all of your emotions, but do so with the calmness of a king. See what your deepest and most raw emotions are, and then take control of them so that you can live like the king of cups does.

The Cards of the Minor Arcana: The Meaning of Swords

Swords: It probably comes as no surprise that the suit most aligned to hardship and struggle is swords. After all, the sword has been the cause of and the settler of countless struggles throughout history. These cards come up most often when there are hardships in your life that you need to overcome. The theme of swords ranges much wider than the other suits, and it covers issues ranging from anger to death and destruction, as well as loss and sorrow. They are thought of as being attuned to the autumn season and the air. Some believe that when swords show up, they help to sharpen a person's awareness and help them cut to the truth of their problems.

Ace: The ace of swords is a connection to the motivating force that pushes you forward through life. This sword is one that represents hope and a chance at success. It often appears when you are starting a new project or escaping from another. If you draw it, then you should remember that you have the strength to take on the challenges ahead. Always hope for the best, not dread and fear the worst.

Two: This card represents the need to make a decision. If you draw it, then remember that the two of swords is misunderstood. People most commonly think that the two of swords means that you have to make a decision now. But this card is patient and understands the value in gathering information before acting.

Three: Lovers all across the world dread this card. It represents heartbreak and the pain of losing someone dear to us. Drawing the three of swords might mean that you are going to have to face sadness in the near future, though it often shows itself when you are already going through your pain. When you see this card, you may want to run from everything that you are doing, but it is telling you to accept it and let the pain come. It will leave soon, and you will be stronger for it.

Four: The four of swords represents rest, and it reminds us that we need to take the time to rest if we want to keep producing, succeeding, or winning at the goals we set. When you draw the four of swords, it means that it's time to take a vacation, catch up on rest, and get back in touch with that quiet place inside yourself.

Five: Conflict brings tension, and the five of swords understands this well. This card reminds us that every fight we have comes at a cost. We don't only lose when we fail, but we also lose when our success costs us something near and dear. Winning an argument doesn't help if you insulted the other person to do it. When you draw this card, you should stop and consider if the cost of your success is damaging those around you.

Six: This card represents leaving behind a painful or harmful situation. Sometimes the only answer we have is to turn around and walk away. We can't beat every challenge, after all. It might fill us with fear, regret, or sadness when we walk away, but it is necessary, so remember this when you draw this card.

Seven: Deception is a part of the world around us. It doesn't necessarily have to be a bad thing, though we often consider it as such. The seven of swords is our connection to that deception, and drawing it tells us that we need to consider if there is a deception that we have fallen for.

Eight: Sometimes, there is nothing to do but weather the storm. We can't find shelter around us, and so we need to keep going through an uncomfortable experience until we can finally do something to make it better. That can be a hurtful thing to accept, but once we understand this, we can keep walking forward without letting it get us down. This card reminds us that we have to let go of our constant need to be free. Once we do, we find that the chains that bound us weren't so tight after all.

Nine: We face anxiety all the time. We're afraid of failure, of success, of losing, of winning. We often lose ourselves to these fears, and they can make us feel like we don't matter. The nine of swords reminds us that these feelings come and go and that we don't need to let them continue to upset us.

TAROT FOR BEGINNERS

Ten: The ten of swords represents the end, the breaking point, the moment where there is no way to retreat, no way back. This might mean the end of a relationship, issues with money, or words that can't be unsaid. When you see the ten of swords, remember that you can't go back and so you shouldn't let the past hold you down. Focus on moving forward instead.

Page: The page of swords is a character of action. This page is always in motion, ready to move with a smile on his face. He has access to all of the knowledge he needs to find success, and so the page of swords understands that he has to act to actualize it. When you draw the page of swords, remind yourself to act as he does.

Knight: The knight of swords is like the page of swords but even more ready for action. He isn't afraid of anything, knowing he is armored in his will power and mental strength. The knight of swords tells us it is time to push ourselves forward with more gusto.

Queen: The queen of swords is a decisive lady that understands what she wants out of life. She doesn't need to lie or cheat her way to it; instead, she chooses honesty and kindness. Such behavior never comes at the cost of her independence, as she has no interest in the whims of others. Drawing the queen of swords is a reminder to be true to ourselves and not what others want us to be.

King: The king of swords is a symbol of wisdom. He is free from the struggles of emotion, and looks at the world with logic and the knowledge of a wizened hero. He may be considered cold, but he doesn't try to be; he is merely confident and secure in himself. When you draw him, he reminds us of this strength inside of ourselves and how we can use it to lead and guide others.

The Cards of the Minor Arcana: The Meaning of Coins

Coins: Coins are often referred to as pentacles. Either label works well for them, as this suit is most concerned with material objects and the physical world. Materials may be actual coins, as in the case of wealth, or they may be objects and items purchased and obtained throughout life. Some consider our love for material objects to be a rein that holds us back, and thus pentacles serves as an apt descriptor in the place of coins. This suit is most tightly related to the winter and the element of earth. Drawing a coin is a sign that there is something that needs your attention, not inside of yourself but in the world outside. Listen to the cards to use your attention wisely.

Ace: As with all aces, the ace of coins represents a beginning as well. That is the beginning of the life that you have worked hard to gain and achieve. These will be your first steps, and you mustn't forget them. If you draw the ace of coins, seek support, and prepare to push forward.

Two: The two of coins represents a change coming. Like the wheel of fortune, the two of coins show us that success and failure are linked, and that one being up means the other is down, but they're always coming back around. If you draw this card, then realize that change is coming, and it can't be stopped.

Three: This card represents intelligence of the highest form. A triumph of genius is in the works, but it needs time for it to come together. When you draw this card, you should know that you are doing well, but you should never forget to plan, consider, and contemplate your actions with intelligence rather than act from a place of ignorance or rashness.

Four: This card represents the fact that all material goods we acquire will fade and go away in time. Possibly that's a scary experience for many to face, but remembering that what comes also goes can be quite good for us. When we draw this card, we shouldn't forget that our material wealth will fade if we aren't careful, and so we should take measures to protect ourselves and our possessions.

Five: This card represents the ideas of desire and of being grateful for what we have. Getting something that we desire fills us with a sense of gratitude, but also one that fades in time. Drawing this card reminds us that while we are happy with money and material goods, we shouldn't confuse this happiness with real, deep-seated happiness.

Six: This card represents generosity, though generosity that comes at a price. This card tells us that getting and giving are not separate events, but two parts of the same coin. When you give, you receive. When you take, you lose. Drawing the six of coins is a sign that you must show and share with others.

Seven: This is another card that reminds us that hard work is required if we want to profit. We like to look for an easy route through struggles and hardships, but the truth of the matter is that we need to work hard.

Drawing this card reminds us that it's this labor that will bring us our successes.

Eight: This card is used to represent improvement. If you draw the eight of coins, then you know that you need to continue working on yourself, your skills, your relationships, or whatever else that position of the spread was related to.

Nine: Dealing with material goods, it is no surprise that the nine of coins is all about financial security. We all want to have money without worries or fears, and that is what this card represents. Drawing it points you towards the work that needs to be done to find this security in your life.

Ten: The ten of coins represents the results of all that hard work. The wealth, respect, and pleasures that we achieve from our hard work are all included in this card, and drawing it is a reminder that your goals don't happen overnight. You will need to put the time in to actualize them.

Page: Young and ready to tackle the world, the page of coins believes he has everything he could ever want. The page of coins knows he can take his winnings and double them, and he can meet any challenge. But he does this because he seeks knowledge and understanding. When you draw him, slow down your plans and seek your own knowledge.

Knight: This knight is the most peaceful of the four suits, as he spends his time worrying about growth rather than action. This knight knows that skills grow on top of each other, that relationships grow, and that plans and actions have wide-ranging consequences that develop with time. Drawing him is a reminder to look at how these actions ripple out and affect the whole.

Queen: The queen of coins loves to solve problems, and drawing her is a sign that you can find answers to your difficulties in her peace and her goodwill.

King: The king of coins has lots of material and spiritual wealth to show the world. He has followed the path of the coins and has acquired more than he could have ever dreamed of. This brings influence and respect, but the king of coins knows that to keep power, you must be careful with it. Drawing the king of coins should serve as a reminder to keep working and to walk the path of strength and respect.

TAROT FOR BEGINNERS

Chapter Summary

- There are 78 cards in a deck of tarot cards. 22 of these are in the major arcana, and 56 of them are in the minor arcana.

- The major arcana are numbered 0-21.

- The fool represents the start of the journey that is the tarot cards, and so the major arcana are sometimes known as the fool's journey.

- The magician represents that special skill that is inside all of us.

- The high priest is our consciousness.

- The empress is connected to mother nature and love.

- The emperor rules over his empire much as we rule over life.

- The hierophant is our connection to our spirituality.

- The lovers are all about connection.

- The chariot is the engine of motivation inside of us.

- Justice is universal justice on a cosmic level.

- The hermit reminds us to seek solitude to answer questions.

- The wheel of fortune continues to turn, just like our fortunes come and go.

- Strength reminds us that we have the power to push through hardship and keep going.

- The hanged man tells us we need to set ourselves right, and that doing so often comes at a cost.

- Death is a reminder that all things end, but that where one thing ends, another can start.

- Temperance reminds us we need to be patient to get to the answer.

- The devil represents the ways we get trapped inside ourselves.

- The tower is a sad card because it represents a burning structure, project, or relationship that can't be fixed.

- The star represents hope and new beginnings.

- The moon is the subconscious.

- The sun tells us to keep going in the same direction.

- Judgment reminds us there is a cosmic karma.

- The world is the end of the tarot deck, and represents the coming together of all the lessons of the tarot into one actualized person.

- There are four suits of the minor arcana: wands, cups, swords, and coins.

- Each suit has an ace, two, three, four, five, six, seven, eight, nine, ten, page, knight, queen, and king.

- The wand suit is related to fire, artisans, creativity, and engineering. The cards in this deck are mostly related to creativity and how it helps us to overcome challenges.

- The cup suit is connected to the spirit inside of us all and helps us gain understanding of questions of the heart and emotions.

- The sword suit is about getting through hardship and dealing with struggle; it points us towards ways that we can fix our problems.

- The coin suit is related to material goods. Drawing cards from it points us towards answers in the realm of the physical, outer world.

In the next chapter, you will learn a few of the most common spreads from three-card spreads that can be used for almost anything, and complex spreads to answer questions of the heart and the career.

CHAPTER FIVE

COMMON TAROT SPREADS

Now that you know what the cards mean, you can start to lay them down and read them correctly. You can always do an intuitive reading and let the cards guide you, but 90% of the time that tarot cards are used, they're done in a spread. There are thousands of spreads that you can discover and learn to use. If you can't find one that works for you, you are always free to make your own. For the time being, let's take a look at some of the most common tarot spreads that are quick and easy to learn and perfect for beginners.

Three-Card Spreads

Three-card spreads are the easiest to learn and perform. You assign three spots in a line one after the other. The first card is laid down slightly to the reader's left. To the right of that, the second card is laid down. The third card is laid down to the right of the second. With that, you have the template for a three-card spread. You can take this to pretty much limitless possibilities. We'll cover five different three-card spreads that you can start using in minutes.

One great three-card spread that can help us to get a better sense of ourselves is the end / start / keep it up spread. The first card pulled tells us what we need to end. That could be an action that is holding us back, or a way in which our actions and attitudes have been hurting another. The second card is what we need to start doing. That will help us to repair the damage from what we had to stop. The final card is the keep it up card. When we find out that we need to end something, we often get hurt by this, and we forget that we are also doing a lot of good. This third card tells us the good that we've been doing and need to maintain. This spread lets us get a better sense of how we should behave, and how we should treat each other and ourselves as we move through life.

If you have a problem, then one of the best spreads is the situation / problem / advice spread. There are many similar spreads that help readers to get a better sense of the problem they are facing, but this one is particularly useful because it doesn't only look at the problem, but also takes into account the situation. Problems arise from, and as parts of, situations and not just as entities unto themselves. This spread starts by laying a card down to get a better sense of the situation, and only then does it move onto figuring out the nature of the problem and the method that will provide the cure. This will leave you not only with a way to approach the problem, but a better understanding of how the problem came to be in the first place.

If you are looking to get more in tune with yourself, then try a mind / body / spirit layout. If you are feeling lost or unsure of where you stand in the world, then this spread is perfect. The first card represents your mind, the next your body, and the third your spirit. Depending on what cards are drawn, you may find a way to get back in touch with each of these elements, or you may find you have not been acting in accordance with your beliefs. You may also find out what forces are preventing you from feeling comfortable in your skin again. Readings of this sort often come up with surprising results because what we believe ourselves to be, and what we really are, are rarely the same. If you approach a mind / body / spirit spread while tangled up in your ego, then you are more likely to avoid the truth the cards show you. Try to approach your readings with an open mind and soul, receptive to the knowledge you discover. Remember that knowledge is impartial, and so it doesn't always correspond to our hopes or beliefs.

If you are like me, then you are into heavy planning and have a schedule set up well ahead of time. If you like to set goals and aim for them, then you can get some advice for tackling these from the tarot deck. Using a now / want / how spread can be a great way to include the tarot in your planning. The first card helps you to get a sense of where you are now. The want card indicates the path you must learn and walk if you are to get to your goal. The how card tells you how you can get to that place, what skills and strengths you have that (if followed) will allow you to achieve your goal.

Finally, a strength / weakness / advice spread is another great way to get a sense of who you are in the present moment and what you are best at. We are often told to follow our strengths and let these guide us, but sometimes we can lose sight of what they are. That's especially true if we can't see a way to direct our strength to the current situation. A great soccer player might not be able to see how his skills on the field will help him when it comes to investing, but there are many skills we don't realize we have. That soccer player had to learn how to train and push themselves, and this sets them up for learning skills like investing. If you aren't sure what strengths you bring to your current situation, draw your first card to find out. Your second card will show you your weakness. The third is the advice card, which here offers a way of making your weakness into a strength itself.

Love Spreads

Love is one of the great mysteries of our existence. Why we love and how we develop it makes about as much sense to the average person as it does to neuroscientists. Love is such an ethereal and confusing experience that it should come as no surprise that easily 50% of the questions tarot readers get are related to love in some way. Love or careers, they're the two biggies. We'll look at careers in a moment, but right now is the time for matters of the heart. We'll look at a couple of wonderful love spreads that you can use, starting with a three-card spread that builds off our previous conversation. Don't worry; we'll be getting up to seven-card spreads with this category, so we're going to give our skills a new challenge.

The easiest way to do a reading on love is to start with three cards and go from there. Do a me / them / dynamic spread. The first card represents who you are. What do you bring to the relationship? Is this what you actually bring, or have you gotten lost in misconceptions of your role? The second card represents your lover. It tells you what role they play while reminding you to consider if this is based in reality or your perceptions, and it asks you to consider how this spirals out to have an influence on your relationship. To get a better understanding of that relationship, we draw the third card. This card represents the dynamic of the relationship and helps you to get a sense of where its core is based. Knowing this allows you to stoke that core to keep the fires of love burning bright.

A more complicated spread is the five-card love spread. Here you have me / them / past / present / future. That is is a great card for getting a sense of where your relationship has been and where it is going. However, the cards are laid out in a slightly odd fashion. The first card is laid to the left like you were starting a three-card spread. The second card jumps the middle card that hasn't been laid yet so that the second card you play would be the final slot of a three-card spread. The third card is placed above the empty middle. The fourth card fills in the middle, and the fifth is laid to the bottom.

This gives a very basic cross shape that can be used for many different spreads. But we're looking at a love spread, so let's get a sense of this.

The first card, laid to the far left, is the me card. That represents what you bring to the relationship and how you act. The second card, on the far right, represents your partner and what they bring to the relationship. The third card, the topmost position of the spread, represents the past which you have come from. The past is where the roots of the relationship are planted. Those roots are strong and grew up together for a reason; this card helps us to get back to that initial attraction and connection. The fourth card, in the middle, is the present. It is *now*, as of the reading, and it will tell you if the relationship is doing well or not. The bottom card is the fifth, and it is the immediate future for the relationship. Each of the four directions has an influence on the middle card, and so you can understand the middle card, the now you are living in, by realizing how each of the four pieces that influence it interact.

Our most complicated spread yet is called a compatibility spread. This spread helps you see how you and your partner interact and connect. There are pieces of interpersonal connection that we often miss in our conscious experience. Turning to the tarot deck can make this much easier. This spread isn't easy, however, as it uses seven cards to represent your wants / their wants / how you differ / how you are alike / if you are emotionally compatible / if you are physically compatible / if you are mentally compatible. To do this, the spread puts the first card down in the left position. Jump the middle and put the second card down to the far right of the first card. The third card is placed underneath the first card, and the fourth card is placed underneath the second. The fifth card is placed between the first and the second card. Place the fifth card so that it rests higher on the table than the first or the second, with the bottom half of the fifth card ending another in the middle of the first and second. Put the sixth card under the fifth, so that it's top half is halfway up the first and the second cards, and its bottom half is halfway down the third and fourth cards. Put the seventh and final card below the sixth so that its top half is halfway up the third and fourth cards. That will give you three columns lined up with two - three - two cards in them.

The first card you lay down represents what you want in a relationship, while the second card that is across from it is what your partner wants. The third card is your differences, and it helps you to understand where you are the most dissimilar. Perhaps that is a deal-breaker in the relationship or merely something to overcome. The fourth card is your similarities. This can help you see where you will bond and agree, but it can also show you that you have similarities that are negative as well. The connection cards make up five, six, and seven, and they let you know if you will be able to connect with each other on the level of your emotions, physicality, and mental prowess.

Career Spreads

Career spreads are among the most difficult of those you will encounter. There are other spreads that are more difficult, but the career spreads have many different unique spreads that will push a beginner's abilities. Considering many variables are involved in our careers, this shouldn't come as any surprise. It is precisely these variables that made us want to consult the tarot deck about our jobs in the first place, after all. We'll look at three spreads ranging from a pyramid to an ill-defined T, and one we use when we face problems in the workplace.

The pyramid spread can be helpful for several kinds of career-based questions. If you are trying to figure out where you should be aiming for the future, then this works, but it also works if you are trying to get a reminder of why you started doing this in the first place. Anytime that you need to get in touch with that profound sense of purpose and planning, a pyramid spread can help. This particular spread works by placing the first three cards in a line like a typical three-card spread. Card four and five are placed above it so that the middle of the card is lined up over the spaces between the first and the second cards and the second and third cards. The sixth and final card is placed at the very top with its middle placed in the space between the fourth and the fifth cards. This spread has the look of a game set up with playing cards rather than tarot cards.

The first card that you lay corresponds to your purpose, your reason for being in this field in the first place. The second card helps you to build on this by connecting you to the source of your motivations. The third card reminds you of your responsibilities and what role you are expected to have. Moving to the next row up, the fourth card is a project check-in. This card is the present; it is for you to get a sense of the environment you are in, and if you still enjoy it or not, if it still excites you in any way. The fifth card is the reward card, and it connects you to what rewards await you if you continue working in this particular career. The sixth and final card is the future, and it tells you where you are headed if you stay on this path. Are you after a career in this field and looking for a promotion, or are you trapped in a field you don't want to be in? Regardless of which is correct, you can find out where you are headed if you stick to this path. This spread might show you that you're going in the right direction, or it might demonstrate that you need a change; either way, you are better equipped with this new-found knowledge.

The next spread looks like an upside-down T, and it is used to get a sense of how we can find achievement. When we know where we want to go, this spread helps us to find a way there. It uses five cards with the first laid in the middle position. The second card is placed beneath the first, and the third is placed beneath the second. The fourth card is placed to the left of the third, while the fifth is placed to the right. That creates two lines of three cards each. These cards begin by helping you get a better sense of your dream job and then work on actualizing it.

The first card is correlated to your dream job. What you pull won't be your dream job itself, but it will give you a sense of how it will make you feel fulfilled and whether or not it is more in tune with the spiritual, the emotional, or the mental. The second card is the road that will lead you there; it tells you what parts of yourself you need to look to for the directions to your goal. The third card helps you to get a sense of how you fit into your dream job. What unique skills and abilities do you bring to the table? Draw and place the third card to find out. The fourth card points you towards the helpers. These might be friends, family, coworkers, strangers, or even parts of yourself. Wherever help rests, the fourth card will point towards it. The fifth and final card is the attention card; it tells you what you have forgotten and what will soon be a problem. When read, you get a solid understanding of how to achieve your career goals.

TAROT FOR BEGINNERS

Our final spread is designed to help solve the problems that crop up again and again in the workplace. It is also the first spread that we've used, which involves laying or stacking cards onto each other. The first card is laid in the middle, and the second card is laid on its side overtop of the first so that it creates the shape of a cross. The third card is placed to the left of this, the fourth card is placed to the right. The fifth card is placed above the first and second, and the sixth card is placed below them. This creates a cross shape which has a smaller cross in its middle. There are many spreads that stack cards above each other, so this shouldn't be considered a radical placement by any stretch of the imagination.

The first card placed represents your goal, the answer you are looking for. In this spread, this is most often the solution to the problem you are trying to deal with. The second card, the one laid over the first, is the challenge that is preventing you from acting. Keep in mind that this card is naturally laying down, and so this can change the way you interpret it. The third card represents what is holding you back and stopping you from being your most efficient. The fourth card is the opposite, and it represents what is pulling you forward and helping you to keep going and being the most productive you can be. The fifth card looks at what you get out of your job. That ranges from the money to the satisfaction to the frustration and disappointment, all and everything that the job provides. The sixth and final card represents the factors that are affecting the entire spread, those elements you can't see directly, but which are impacting and making the problem worse. When you take these all together, you can solve any career-centered problem you face with the wisdom of the tarot.

Chapter Summary

- Spreads are simply ways of arranging the cards in order to get an answer from them.

- Each location in the spread has its meaning, which alters the way the card is to be read.

- The easiest spreads to do are three-card spreads. One card to the left, one in the middle, and one to the right.

- Three-card spreads can be used for just about any topic you can think of, but they won't be able to give you elaborate detail on the topic.

- Common topics for spreads include love and careers.

- There are many spreads with five or more cards, which all interact with each other to produce their complete meaning.

- Practice more difficult spreads first on your own before working them on other people.

- Cards are often laid over the top of each other to create alternative meanings to each other.

In the next chapter, you will learn all the terminology that you've encountered throughout the book and that you'll face once you start talking about tarot cards out there in the real world.

CHAPTER SIX

GLOSSARY

There are a lot of words and terms when it comes to tarot card reading, so, hopefully, this glossary will come in handy. It's packed full of all the weird words you'll find in this book, as well as many that are floating around out there, which we didn't even have time to get into just yet. It's my hope that you'll find this chapter paying off, even after you are well beyond the status of beginner.

Air: The unseeable element, considered to be magical and represented in the minor arcana by the wand suit.

Akasha: Also known as spirit, another intangible element that is considered to be magical, though not directly assigned to a suit.

Altar: Any surface that is set aside for use with only a certain ritual. A priest stands in front of an altar when they give Mass, though this altar is representative of power to those in the Christian faith. An altar can have magical power, though often its power is the personal or spiritual significance the altar has. Some tarot users only read the cards on their altar.

Aquarius: One of the Zodiac signs, for people born between January 21 and February. Said to have a connection to air.

Aries: One of the Zodiac signs, for people born between March 21 and April 20. Said to have a connection to fire.

Baton: The minor arcana suit that we have been referring to as wands.

Cancer: One of the Zodiac signs, for people born between June 22 and July 22. Said to have a connection to water.

Capricorn: One of the Zodiac signs, for people born between December 23 and January 20. Said to have a connection to earth.

Cartomancy: This is the name given to the art of using cards to read the future. This can be done with any type of card, including tarot cards, but it is not directly related to the art of reading tarot card spreads.

Chalice: The minor arcana suit that we have been referring to as cups.

Clubs: The minor arcana suit that we have been referring to as wands. Clubs is the French name, which made its way into modern-day playing cards.

Coins: A suit of the minor arcana. It is known as diamonds in the French, has a connection to earth and merchants, as well as the physical body or your possessions.

Consultant: A tarot card reader is sometimes called a consultant because they "consult the cards" for advice and solutions to your problems.

Court Cards: The page, knight, queen, and king from each minor arcana suit. These correspond loosely to the face cards in a deck of playing cards. They may have different names, and so "court cards" is a catch-all to refer to their position rather than their individual title in a deck.

Cups: A suit of the minor arcana. It is also known as hearts in the French, has a connection to water and the clergy, as well as emotions and love.

Devil's Picture Book: This was a derogatory name given to tarot cards, though in recent years, it has been taken as an ironic badge of honor by many.

Dignified: A term used to describe a card that is placed down in a standing position.

Disks: The minor arcana suit that we have been referring to as cups.

Divination: The art of telling the future through the use of some kind of tool. While cartomancy specifically uses cards, divination can be carried out through casting stones or many other ways. For example, cartomancy is a subtype of divination.

Earth: The ground, trees, and nature. Earth is associated with the suit of coins and is considered one of the elements to hold its own source of magic.

Fire: The flame and the sun. Fire is associated with the suit of wands, and is considered one of the elements to hold its own source of magic.

Fool's Journey: The tarot deck begins with the fool. The fool's journey is a story of the fool traveling through the other 21 cards of the major arcana. It is a fun story to learn, and telling it with the cards can make for a captivating party trick.

Golden Dawn: A group of occultists that studied magic in the Western world. A.E. Waite and P. Coleman Smith met as members and formed two-thirds of the group behind the Rider-Waite tarot deck, as Waite provided the knowledge, and Smith illustrated the cards.

Hearts: The minor arcana suit that we have been referring to as Cups. Hearts is the French name, which made its way into modern playing cards.

Ill Dignified: One way of referring to a card that is played with the front of the card down.

Intuitive Reading: Most of the time, we ask the tarot cards a question and then translate the answer through the cards. An intuitive reading is when you spread the cards without a question in mind and see what they are saying on their own.

Leo: One of the Zodiac signs, for people born between July 23 and August 21. Said to have a connection to fire.

Libra: One of the Zodiac signs, for people born between September 24 and October 23. Said to have a connection to air.

Little White Book: The little white book is a shorthand way of referring to the instructional manual that comes with a set of playing cards. While many decks no longer have a white manual, the most popular ones did, and the nickname stuck.

Major Arcana: The 22 trump cards in the deck that begin with the fool and represent the fool's journey through life and awareness.

Minor Arcana: 56 cards split into four suits of 14 cards, each ranging from ace to king. They are like a normal set of playing cards except that they go 10, page, knight, queen, and king at the end. Each of the 56 cards has its meaning, but, most often, they modify elements of the major arcana.

Numerology: Numerology is a form of divination that sees portents in numbers and believes these have great value in seeing the future. Numerologists may use the tarot deck in their readings, but this is not a normal function of the tarot deck itself.

Oracle Deck: An oracle deck is similar to a tarot deck, but it is more interested in reading peoples' fortunes. Each deck is unique, and they haven't been around nearly as long as tarot cards have either.

Path: Path sometimes refers to the magical path that one walks in one's life, but it can also represent the 22 possibilities of the major arcana.

Pentacles: The minor arcana suit that we have been referring to as coins.

Pip: All the cards of the minor arcana are numbered. Some sets include these numbers, and others require you to memorize the card's meaning. The pip refers to the number of the card itself, and, secondly, the part of the card that it is written on.

Pisces: One of the Zodiac signs, for people born between February 20 and March 20. Said to have a connection to water.

Querent: Divination may be practiced alone, but it is most often practiced with a client or friend that has things they need to know about the future. When this is the case, the person with the questions is the querent.

Reader: The reader is the person who draws the cards, lays the spread, and reads the results.

Reversed Card: A card that is reversed may be upside down or backward, the same as an ill dignified card.

Rods: The minor arcana suit that we have been referring to as wands.

Runes: Dating back much further than the tarot, runes were symbols carved into small but hard surfaces that could be rolled like dice or spread out like cards to perform acts of divination.

Sagittarius: One of the Zodiac signs, for people born between November 23 and December 22. Said to have a connection to fire.

Scepters: The minor arcana suit that we have been referring to as wands.

Significator: When an act of divination is happening through the cards, often, the person asking the question will be given a card that represents them through the rest of the reading. This card becomes the central element, and the others then modify and interact with it.

Spades: The minor arcana suit that we have been referring to as swords. Spades is the French name, which made its way into modern-day playing cards

Spirit: One of the magical elements, along with fire, earth, water, and air.

Spread: The way in which the tarot cards are laid down. Each location of a spread has a particular meaning that affects the meaning of the cards laid down there.

Staves: The minor arcana suit that we have been referring to as wands.

Swords: A suit of the minor arcana. It is also known as spades in the French, has a connection to water and the nobility and the military, as well as reason.

Tarot Cards: The 22 trump cards referred to as the major arcana and 56 cards of the minor arcana, which are split into four suits of 14 cards each. The cards each have a particular meaning and help us to get in touch with our inner wisdom.

Tarot Deck: The tarot deck is the 78 cards made up of the major and minor arcana.

Taurus: One of the Zodiac signs, for people born between April 21 and May 21. Said to have a connection to earth.

Virgo: One of the Zodiac signs, for people born between August 22 and September 23. Said to have a connection to earth.

Wands: A suit of the minor arcana. It is also known as clubs in the French, has a connection to fire and builders, as well as creativity and willpower.

Water: One of the magical elements, along with fire, earth, air, and spirit.

FINAL WORDS

While the tarot deck is surrounded by mystique and mythology, it isn't any more complicated than most card games. But the tarot deck isn't a game, so much as it is a tool for understanding yourself and the wisdom you hold. The tarot deck will point you towards the answers inside of yourself and show you the truths that you didn't want to face. These cards offer advice and wisdom that can let us live a much fuller and more fulfilling life.

The first step to using the tarot deck is to stop giving power to the myths surrounding it. We look at the history of the tarot deck and these myths themselves in the first chapter so that we can cut away all the misunderstandings and get to the core truth at hand. This then set us up so that we could pick our own deck, learn how to ask questions of the deck, and get a sense of how spread and position affect meaning in chapter two.

With a solid understanding of the deck in hand, we turned our attention towards the cards themselves to get a sense of how decks differ from each other, and how the major and minor arcanas function. Since this made up chapter three, chapter four was free to explore the meanings of each and every one of the 78 cards we use as a part of the tarot deck. We can't read the cards until we know the cards, and this chapter is one that you'll want to study until you are comfortable and have integrated the knowledge into a part of yourself.

We closed out on chapter five, where we learned how to do some of the more common spreads in tarot. These ranged from simple three-card spreads to complicated spreads of five or more cards with overlapping cards, and specific rules surrounding placement. Just because these already have rules on how to use them, you shouldn't think anything is holding you back from making your own. Follow what you feel, always.

The thing with the tarot deck is that rules and guidelines are never as important as what you feel and understand to be true in your heart. Your relationship to your cards might look nothing like another reader's, and that is perfectly fine. So long as you respect the cards and understand them, you are free to use them in whatever way they call out to you. I hope that you have learned enough to get started performing your own readings and that I am lucky enough to receive one myself someday.

CRYSTALS FOR BEGINNERS

A Practical Guide to Using Healing Crystals and Stones

By
Abigail Welsh & Edson Keenan

INTRODUCTION

Healing crystals have had a resurgence in popularity recently. The internet has helped this to a large degree, as it has made it easier to find out information on this fascinating topic. The interest in using healing crystals for emotional wellbeing has caught on with celebrities, fashion designers, and adherents of New Age lifestyles. Crystals have taken over Etsy, the online marketplace that specializes in handcrafted, alternative, and custom-made items and gifts. In fact, because Etsy has found them such a fast-selling product, it's been difficult for them to retain any stock. Crystals are very popular with those people who like "mystic beauty," a style of fashion that mixes spirituality with beauty. Examples of mystic beauty products are necklaces or dresses which use healing crystals as part of the design.

Healing crystals first came to the wider public's attention in the 1970s. At that time, what we'd now call New Age philosophies were still developing out of the hectic youth culture experimentation of the 1960s. This made it very easy for people to dismiss these crystals as a bunch of nonsense, or even see them in a sinister light. The late 1960s had seen the optimism of the Summer of Love when young people on America's West Coast converged in attempts to find new spiritual and cultural paths but had then witnessed such ideals perverted by the appalling violence of the Manson "family." It became very easy to disregard anything derived from such sources as escapist or dangerous. The exploration of spirituality and alternative forms of healing slowly faded as the 1970s progressed. By the time the 1980s came around, cultural values had moved fully from spirituality and emotional exploration. By then, the focus was on trickle-down economics and the new war on drugs. Healing crystals faded from the popular consciousness at this time, though there were those who continued to teach of them and sing their praises.

As we've progressed into our modern, technologically connected age, there has been a return to the spirituality of this earlier period. Despite being more connected than ever before, people are experiencing greater loneliness and anxiety than was common in the past. Our brains evolved throughout history in order to allow us to function as communities and tribes. We just aren't supposed to be exposed to so much marketing and advertising. We're not even very good at maintaining a social circle of more than 150 people, including family, friends, neighbors, and coworkers. This modern malaise is responsible for a return to spirituality, and with it has come a reawakening of interest in healing crystals.

Despite being included under the umbrella title of New Age, the use of healing crystals is said to go back throughout most of human history. It is safe to say that we have always found crystals compelling. They were used to show class and rank or to accentuate beauty. As we developed better sciences, we discovered that crystals could be used in electronics and other modern inventions. The use of crystals in science shows us that there are definitely practical uses and purposes that they can be put towards. Most people readily accept that. But when you start to mention crystal healing, you often end up with these same people largely dismissing the idea. These individuals often view crystal healing as a nonsense belief that isn't grounded in science. Or, they might see such ideas as a sign of occult influence, that dark, possibly Satanic, forces are attempting to do harm to the world. This second belief we can dismiss out of hand. There is nothing occult about using healing crystals. There is no dark energy, no evil presence, no Satanic masterplan. But that comment about science brings up an intriguing thread to explore.

CRYSTALS FOR BEGINNERS

If you don't believe that crystals have mythic properties that allow for healing, then I am not about to try to change your mind. However, if you argue that there is no science behind using healing crystals, then I would suggest that is taking far too hasty a view. It is perfectly true that science does not point towards a clear result that states, "These crystals have healing properties, and we should study them more." But science doesn't need to look at healing crystals *directly* to show how they do have power. The findings that tell us the most about healing crystals actually come from drug testing.

When you test a new drug, you don't just give it out to somebody and watch the results. Instead, you gather together a few test groups. You give the new medication to one group, and you give a placebo to the other group. This is known as double-blind testing. The sign that a drug genuinely has potency is when the results show that the group that received it has a higher success rate than those that didn't. But those that didn't still often show the effects of the drug, despite not taking it. This is called the placebo effect, and it ties directly into our use of crystals.

The placebo effect is in and of itself a truly mind-boggling phenomenon. If we are told that we have taken a drug, we expect that drug to begin to work. This expectation or belief then fuels a physical or mental change within our bodies. There was an old prank in my high school where people would pretend to dose others with LSD. They would tell them that they slipped it into their drinks or food. The unfortunate victim would then trip out, and often, they were sent to the nurse's office. Yet there was never any LSD present; it was entirely a lie told for the prank. But the person who was tricked fully believed it, and they would swear that they were hallucinating. The reason this is so fascinating to me is that it demonstrates how our brains have the ability to change how our reality works based on what we believe to be true about reality. Therefore, it can be argued, healing crystals work so long as you believe in them.

You might counter that the placebo effect only shows us that healing crystals don't work at all, that they aren't real. But if the placebo effect can completely alter the lived experience of a person, then how is that anything but real? All we are as we go through this life is our consciousness, so if that can be altered, then reality itself is alterable. Further findings in this direction come from the scientific study of the brain and how it is affected by religion. Scientific research has indicated that people who believe in God experience less pain when they pray. A religious person may ascribe this to divine intervention, though a scientific-minded person would argue for a placebo effect. But, if it is a placebo effect, does this mean that God isn't real?

In a way, healing crystals are the same. If you believe in them, then they are going to work. If you do not believe in them, then they are unlikely to work for you. But if you are on the fence, then it can go either way. However, we can make the active choice to believe in the healing properties of these crystals. When we do this, we ensure that they work for us because we have deemed that reality to be so.

My goal is this book will not be to convince you one way or another that these crystals really work. I am quite sure that they do, and I believe that you agree with me, or you will do so before too long. My goal, however, is to introduce you to the many reasons why people use healing crystals. From there, we will explore the best crystals for healing our emotions and what crystals are most appropriate for beginners. With a solid understanding of all these moving parts, we'll turn our attention to the various ways that we can use healing crystals in our lives and then close out on tips for improving your healing crystal experience. By the time we finish, it is my hope that you will have a deep understanding and appreciation for these remarkable and powerful tools.

CHAPTER ONE

WHY USE HEALING CRYSTALS?

The title of this chapter asks an important question. Just exactly why is it any of us should be worrying about or using healing crystals? The answer to this particular question is not exactly hard to answer. In fact, you'll find that there are many different answers to this question plastered all over the internet. But the plethora of answers also brings with it a problem: Which are right?

Unfortunately, this isn't one of those issues which has a single simple answer. There is no one reason to use healing crystals. There are dozens upon dozens. Some of these uses seem to go together quite well and make it easy to see the way they interact with each other. But then there are those answers which seemingly contradict other answers. If you believe that there is one solid answer as to why you should use healing crystals, then you are going to wind up somewhat frustrated with the whole ordeal.

In order to give this question enough room to be properly answered, I have collected together many of the different reasons people use healing crystals. These range from seeking balance and calming the emotions to stepping out of the electromagnetic field, finding pain relief, romance, or even detoxifying your home. You'll notice that these range from the purely psychological to the entirely mystical. I'd like to give you a full understanding of the topic, rather than one that simply dismisses or wholly embraces the mystical realm. Each of us has our own spiritual beliefs and ideals. Rather than try to convince you of a spiritual concept, this approach will let you investigate it for yourself to decide if crystal healing is right for you.

Getting in Touch With Your Emotions

Many of us go through life as a slave to our emotions. If we are happy, then we think that life is wonderful, but when we're sad or anxious, we think that life is horrible, that it only wants to hurt us and that it never did anything good for anyone. If you believe in chakras, then you may see this as a sign that your chakras are clogged up, but most people don't have this disconnection from their own emotional experience. Instead of seeing their emotions as something that *happens* to them, they see emotions as an intrinsic part of themselves. We all tend to do this, to over-identify with our emotions instead of regarding them as transient phenomena. Getting lost in our emotions can be very scary, but healing crystals can help us out a lot in this area.

Different crystals have different purposes. There are those that help with romance, those that help with pain, some that help to calm us, and some that improve our concentration. We'll be looking at these in more depth throughout the book, but the range of uses points towards our emotional experiences. How can we be calm if we are lost in our emotions? As we'll see, we can turn to a healing crystal.

Regardless of how you use your crystals (which we cover in depth in chapter four), one of the powerful things about them is the way that they take on meanings of their own. For example, we use amethyst to help us deal with our anxiety or sadness. If we find that we are overly irritable, then we'll use some jade. If we have too much stress, we can use the gorgeous moonstone to help us let it go. These are just a few of the available crystals we use for emotional purposes, but how do they help us?

We'll be using the word intention a lot throughout the book. For our purposes right now, an intention is simply the purpose that we intend our crystals to serve. So, if you are stressed, then you would take a moonstone and set the intention as stress relief. As you gather more crystals around you, you'll come to have one or two each for most of your emotions that you need help dealing with. When you feel the negative emotion, you then turn to your healing crystals rather than get lost in it. Whether it is the crystal itself or the intention that you set, which helps you to deal with the feeling, the result is the same. You create a space between yourself and your emotional experience and then use crystals to alter and change it.

Practicing with healing crystals is a fantastic way to learn more about your own emotions. They also offer a wonderful way of getting in touch with your reactions and responses. You need first to identify that you are upset before you can turn to your healing crystals to help you manage it. This act of identifying your emotional experience is one of the most effective ways of understanding your own emotions and thus being able to conquer them.

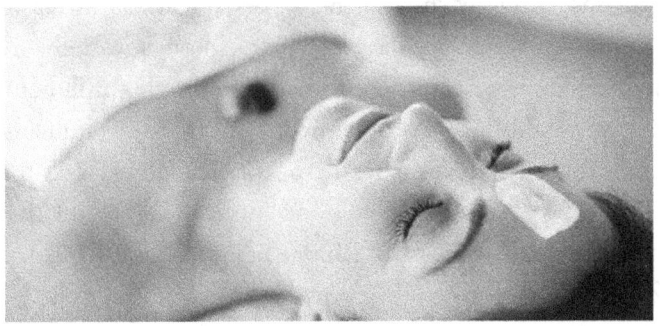

Seek Balance

We mentioned chakras in the last section, so let's continue with them for a moment. If you believe in chakras, then you know that they are situated throughout your body, and each one acts almost like a gate. If they are open, then healing energy can flow through them. When your chakras are open, you have a great sense of peacefulness and contentment. But problems start to occur when they get closed or blocked up. In fact, if you believe in their significance, most of the emotional and mental problems that we experience are explained through chakras

Everything in the world is made up of frequencies, primarily electromagnetic, and crystals are no different here. However, different crystals have a different frequency, and this is what makes them better or worse for a particular use. We are said to have seven different chakras, and each of these reacts to a different frequency. We might have problems in our lower chakra and find that we can't find romance or sexual fulfillment. Or we might have a problem with our throat chakra and find that we never speak up for ourselves, ask the questions we need to know, or speak in a manner that touches the depths of our inner being. When this is the case, we can turn to different crystals. For example, we might wear a necklace with lapis lazuli in it so we can unblock our throat chakra.

If you are finding that you feel like you are out of balance in your life and in your mind, then you may want to consider exploring your chakras. A healing crystal could help you in this matter so that you can live your life as the most activated and honest version of yourself possible.

Romance and Sexual Energy

Both romance and sexual energy have chakras assigned to them. Romance is located in the heart, while sexual energy or potency is found in the lower regions just above the genitals. These are two of the spaces which are said to get blocked up the most often. When we are unlucky in love, we can often convince ourselves that we were meant to be alone or that our loneliness is a sign of our worthlessness. There is nothing wrong with a relationship ending or a date going poorly; this is simply the risk involved in any interpersonal relationship. But when we convince ourselves that our love life is a sign of something wrong with us, we clog up our chakras. Or, if you don't believe in chakras, you might interpret this as the way we can get lost in our thoughts, and allow our negativity to spiral out and affect our lives.

One use for healing crystals is to help repair this damage in our hearts. To help us deal with matters of romance, we use a crystal with a pink, orange, or red color. This color alone connects it to the same emotional sphere as love, and this helps us to fuse our intentions into the crystal and our minds. We may choose to wear a low-hanging necklace so that we can keep our healing crystal over our hearts and allow its vibrational frequencies to be closest to our love chakra.

Another issue that we often face is thinking that we are sexually repulsive or too unqualified to pleasure another being. While we might not have much experience, there is no reason that we should feel this way. When two people come together, they need to discover each other's bodies themselves to learn how they work. This is a process filled with errors and mistakes and (hopefully) laughter and love. But we live in a society that tells us how well we should perform, when we should have sex, how long we should be having it for, and all sorts of other weird messages that leads to confusion and can result in us getting bewildered and lost. Rather than live in the experience and enjoy it for what it is, we burden ourselves with anxiety and worries and nervousness, and these can greatly reduce how pleasurable the experience is for both parties.

By infusing a healing crystal with sexual energy, we can break free from the messages we have been told, and, instead, get back in touch with the act itself. You may want to meditate with your crystal before performing, or you may want to wear it on a bracelet or something similar. By setting your intention ahead of time, connecting with this crystal becomes a way of tapping into the limitless libido inside of us all.

It should be noted that healing crystals used for matters of love don't just refer to the type of romantic love between two people. These crystals can also be a great way to get in touch and rediscover a love for yourself. If you are having a hard time accepting who you are or if you don't love yourself yet, then a healing crystal with an intention of love might be exactly what you need.

Improve Psychic Powers

You don't need to be a psychic to get benefits from using healing crystals. This is a common myth that is common around many of the practices that have come to be known as New Age. The perfect example of this is tarot cards, as they are one of the most widely known of these practices. But just like tarot cards, healing crystals are more often used for the psychological benefits that they provide rather than psychic ones. Just like tarot cards, healing crystals can be used for psychic purposes, though this is not their most common use. It is like using a spoon as a fork, it can do what you want, but it wasn't intended for this purpose.

Those with psychic powers may use amethyst or apophyllite to activate and strengthen their third eye, that psychic eye that exists inside the forehead and the brain. The crystals are given the intention of improving your psychic abilities, and then they are typically worn as part of a decorative headband, or they are placed on the forehead during meditation. The vibrations from these crystals help to open up and clear out the third eye so that your psychic visions will be more powerful.

Improve Your Skin

While some of us aren't especially bothered, most of us want to have beautiful and healthy-looking skin that is clear from blemishes and other unattractive features. The populations of affluent countries spend millions upon millions of dollars on skincare products, not just every year but every single quarter. New products come out all the time with the latest scientifically formulated mixture to ensure that your skin looks wonderful. But, instead of turning to these endlessly new creations, perhaps we could benefit from turning towards something a little bit older. It has been this idea that has driven the market of healing crystals used in skincare products.

There have been quite a few products of late that use small pieces of crystal to ensure beautiful skin. One example is the Gemstone Organic Rose Quartz Creme, which uses rose quartz as well as smoky quartz and kunzite. Another product is the Tracie Martyn Complexion Savior, which includes a little bit of malachite. Of course, it should be clear that these use healing crystals as part of their overall product and not as the product itself. This brings into question whether or not the crystals have anything to do with improving the skin at all. It could just be that the pharmaceutical ingredients do all the work.

In that case, what about a face roller that uses jade? These have been around for quite some time, and they are known to help reduce the puffy appearance of skin. Not only that, but they leave a noticeable shine to the skin that suggests that they help bring the natural oils to the surface. This is further backed up by the fact that jade rollers help the skin to absorb creams and other rub-on products. That's made possible by the way jade helps to open the pores of the skin. So next time you are thinking about purchasing some facial cream or other skincare products, consider adding healing crystals to your routine.

Help Plants Grow

This is one of the many uses that healing crystals have around the house. Some people like to bring healing crystals into the home for decorative purposes, but others use them in a more thoughtful manner (such as for feng shui, covered next). This particular use is one that stands outside of any science that I know of, including that of the placebo effect. Simply put, plants don't have the neurological component necessary for the placebo effect to work. It may be that adding crystals to a plant provokes the placebo effect in the owner, as they see the crystal as doing the work rather than the plant's environment and biology. But when looking for more information on this particular use, it becomes clear that it is tightly tied to psychic explanations.

There is a tendency to think of psychics as having the ability to see into the future or perceive the possible threads of fate as they are weaved together. This is most obvious in jokes made at the expense of psychics such as "If you're psychic, then you should know who's calling." But what these miss is that a psychic isn't necessarily able to see into the future, so much as they work from and through emotions, intuition, and other unseen elements of understanding. One of the things that is often reported is that psychics have a strong connection to nature, or they have an intuitive sense as to the needs of Mother Nature. It is this connection that leads us to the use of healing crystals in raising plants.

Crystals are added to the soil or to the container housing the plant. The plant's vibrational frequencies should be in the same range as the crystal. This needs to be discovered intuitively, and some psychics suggest asking your plants which crystals they want to use. Add the crystal and watch as the plant begins to thrive.

Aid in Feng Shui

Chakras are one of the ways that we explain and understand the emotional and spiritual experiences that we are having as we go about our lives. They play on the unseen energies that affect and move us all. Each of us is a world unto ourselves, and this means that we bring our energies with us no matter where we go. But there is also environmental energy; unseen forces which lend power to the places we occupy. If you have ever walked into a room and immediately felt a negative energy, then you know first-hand the way that locations can take on and store their own emotional and intangible vibrational energy.

One way that we cleanse and balance these environmental energies is through the use of feng shui. Rather than living at odds with the environmental energy around us, feng shui gives us a way of smoothing out our experience so that the energy of the environment and the energy that we bring can coexist without clashing. Feng shui practices range from the way you position furniture to how often you clean your windows, as well as what objects you bring into the house. Some of the objects that we can use to increase our feng shui are healing crystals.

These stones represent a form of energy taken from the earth. They are energy collected into a physical form that you can then use with care and consideration to assist in your life and your feng shui. Just as these crystals can be used to balance our emotions, they can be used to help us balance the energies of our home. But to this end, it is important that we keep in mind that each crystal has a different purpose and power. It doesn't help our feng shui out if all we do is place crystals around the house in a haphazard and unconsidered manner. If you were placing heaters in your house, you wouldn't just toss them anywhere. You would consider each room and where the best location to put them is and how much heat you need in a particular space. Healing crystals should be used in this manner, considered and placed carefully to achieve an effect rather than left to the chaos of indifference.

The most commonly used crystal in feng shui is the jade crystal. This crystal is said to bring good luck to the owner and makes the home into a luckier space. It also represents the possibility of new beginnings, so it is a particularly great crystal to begin with, in the sense of starting to use crystals as a beginning in and of itself. Jade is also said to bring fortune into the household, and so it is commonly paired with the money bonsai as a gift since both are meant to bring riches. Also used often is clear quartz, which helps to remove the negative energies from around the home. Rose quartz is also quite popular since it represents love. If you are married, then rose quartz is used to help strengthen the relationship and create a loving energy in the home. Remember that these are just a few examples of how healing crystals are used in feng shui, I'm sure you'll discover plenty more yourself.

Pain Relief

Pain can cripple us and steal away our lives. Or, at least, it can make it feel that way. If you experience chronic pain, then you know first-hand how debilitating it can be. You might have a thousand things you need to get done, but if you're in too much pain, then there's no way you're going to get out of bed. If you experience anything that brings a lot of pain into your reality, then you've probably looked for ways to treat it. While modern medicine has achieved wonders in this field, there is still a lot of work that needs to be done. I can't begin to tell you how many people I've met that have been prescribed opiates despite not wanting them. It seems that our main way of dealing with pain is through dangerously addictive chemical concoctions. I don't want to suggest that these have no value, but they do have many negative side-effects, and this puts many people off using them.

Healing crystals offer us another way of dealing with our pain, and there are tons of people who swear by them. Whether it was their natural frequencies that helped out or it was the placebo effect, the fact of the matter is that many people have found pain relief through using crystals. They are not the kind of thing that would be recommended by doctors, but they can help. Rather than claim them to be better or worse than medication, please make sure you seek out a professional medical opinion in conjunction with their use rather than relying solely on the crystals. With that said, let's take a quick look at some of the crystals that people use to take their lives back from pain.

Amethyst is often called the master healer, and it is considered to be the most effective crystal in treating pain. It has a very high frequency of vibration that makes it appropriate for treatment of pains such as arthritis or headaches. It is also used to treat stress. Cortisol, the stress hormone, can make pain worse, so this is doubly beneficial. Lapis lazuli is also recommended for pain relief, though it only has minor healing properties that make it best for smaller pains. What lapis lazuli has going for it is the fact that it helps to strengthen the mind, and this can make us better at withstanding and putting up with pain. Hematite is used to help with the flow of blood through the body, and it is worn to reduce blood pressure and other issues that can make your veins feel like they are filled with fire. Rose quartz is used in the treatment of skin, not only as a cosmetic, but also to reduce the pain from burns and inflammatory issues. If you've got a sunburn, use a little rose quartz along with your aloe vera to help lower the level of pain overall.

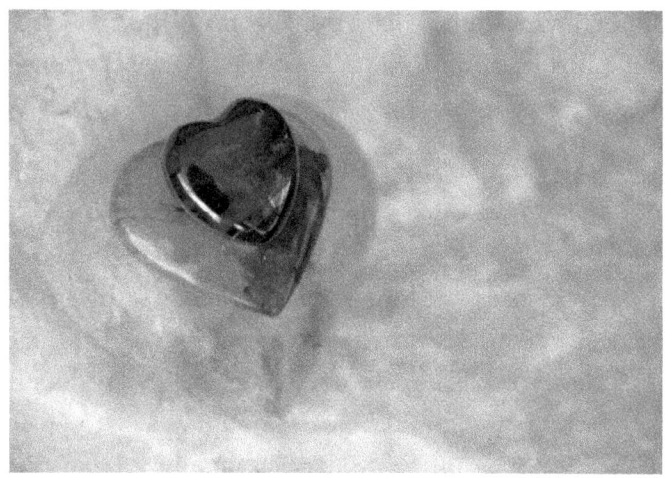

Increase Your Happiness

We already talked about how healing crystals can help you to get in touch with your emotions. This same feature has a bi-product of helping you to understand your own happiness in a much fuller sense. But this isn't the only way in which healing crystals improve and increase our happiness. There are many different crystals that are said to have healing powers, and we'll briefly glance at those here, but, first, there is a more mundane consideration we need to take into account. Simply put: crystals are attractive.

One of the reasons that crystals became so popular was because of their gorgeous looks. They can have bold bright colors, or they could be clear or even entirely dark. Some shine, others let light pass through them. They all have different textures and feelings, and these can make them quite enjoyable to hold in your hand. The beautiful nature of these crystals tends to spark reflection and to bring the mind into a pleasant state as you consider their beauty. One of the best things we can do for our happiness is take in beautiful things such as nature or art, and crystals are another of these beautiful objects we can use to improve our sense of wellbeing.

Moving on from crystals as a whole, we find that there are many different healing crystals that are said to have ties to the emotional sphere of happiness. The amazonite is said to bring joy through the way it helps us discover and listen to our inner thoughts and feelings. We each have an inner truth, a way that we want to live. This isn't the same as an ambition like, "I want to be a successful writer or actor." Instead, this is more like, "I want to be a good person and to bring positivity to those around me." This is a deeper truth. Unfortunately, we often have a hard time connecting to such truths, and thus we live our lives as we are told we should and not as we genuinely want to deep inside. Amazonite can help us to connect to this truth. In doing so, it helps us to live more honestly and fully and to appreciate those around us, as well as ourselves.

Citrine is a beautiful, bright yellow crystal. If we look at citrine, it is hard not to think of the sun and the brightness of day, or the warm feeling that comes from bathing in its rays. This stone brings a feeling of being carefree and makes us more likely to take actions that put us outside of our comfort zone. While this may sound - pardon the pun - uncomfortable, psychologists have discovered that we are at our happiest when we are trying new things and pushing ourselves to achieve more.

Tiger's eye is another crystal with connotations of nature and the sun. Its tiger-striped colors bring in lots of browns as well, and this evokes a lovely feeling of nature, of the forests and trees that provide us with our oxygen and thus our ability to live in the first place. This helps us to tap into that primal center inside of us all so that we can find strength and courage to take on whatever life throws at us.

You might be noticing a pattern with these three crystals. While some are said to bring happiness directly, many crystals don't actually do this. What they do is to help bring balance across our whole so that we can more easily find happiness. They help us to reduce our stress so that we can live happier. They help us to push outside of our familiar routines so that we can be more inventive and energetic. They help us to tap into our internal strength so that we can discover more about ourselves. All these are avenues to find happier lives. They don't directly affect happiness, but they affect the factors that help contribute to happiness in a positive way.

Tap Into Calmness

One of the things that has already begun to crop up frequently throughout this book is the way that our modern world isn't designed to facilitate our emotional needs. Nowhere is this more clear than when we look at the idea of calmness. Have you noticed how everything seems to happen faster and faster these days? We have a 24/7 news cycle, and our social media feeds never ever end; they just scroll on forever. Commercials are edited to overload our senses, and we're constantly fighting traffic jams, balancing our finances, and trying to get promoted. All of this tells us to go, go, go, but it doesn't consider what this is doing to our psyches. Our constant need to push forward and keep moving, keep aiming for what's next, keep up with the news, and stay active online all cause us lots of stress. We don't always notice that we have this stress because we're so bombarded with it that we've come to think it is normal.

But then it comes time for bed, and we find ourselves unable to sleep. We're restless. We've been told to go faster and faster, to do more and more, to take in more information. But we're never told to relax and calm down, and take time away to get back in touch with ourselves, to seek out a piece of calm within us. This message has been so readily ignored that many of us think that calmness is a bad thing.

But if we want to live a healthy life, then we need to find a calm center in ourselves. This will lower our anxiety, improve our happiness, and increase our life expectancies. But with so many of us unsure of how to go about it, it can be hard to achieve. Thankfully, there are healing crystals that can help us here.

Amethyst, hematite, and moonstone are just three types of healing crystals that help to create a sense of calm. Their energies are very mild. This doesn't mean that they aren't potent, but they help us in a way that isn't explosive or over the top. They do the exact opposite; they soothe us instead of stimulating us. These calming energies can be felt when worn as jewelry, but the most effective approach is to combine calming crystals with meditation or even a bath. These activities already help to promote a sense of calm that grows exponentially when combined with the use of a healing crystal picked and imbued for this purpose.

Protection from Negative Energies

One of the ways that we protect ourselves from negative energies is by seeking understanding and balance in our emotional realm. Another way is to use feng shui to make our living environment into a more relaxed and positive place. But these are just two ways in which we bring positivity into our lives. To use a stretched metaphor, this kind of protection is like purchasing a gun. It can bring with it a sense of protection, but it doesn't do anything to prevent intruders. Likewise, when we balance our emotions or use feng shui, we are increasing our happiness, but we aren't preventing the negative from entering our lives. To complete the metaphor, we don't need a gun. We need a fence.

We built a fence up around our happiness, and this protects us from negativity. We might still encounter negativity in our lives, but our fence keeps it at a distance. We aren't opening our doors and inviting it in. We can see it, recognize it for what it is, and then go back inside and continue to be content. Since we're talking about happiness and negativity, there are no real fences. But we can use healing crystals to give us an assist in this manner.

Some healing crystals are said to be used for protection such as fire agata, black obsidian, or fluorite. Adding these stones to your home, or to your jewelry, can help to give you this protection. Whether the stones do it themselves, or they function on the placebo effect again, the result is the same. You become more aware of the way that you interact with negativity, and this helps you to distance yourself from it. Knowing that you are protected, you can see the negativity without looking through the eyes of fear.

If you want the most protection possible, then a bracelet or necklace with multiple crystals is the way to go. But don't just use stones that are meant for protection. Instead, use a protection stone and then a happiness stone, another protection stone, and then a stone for health. By combining these, you create a piece of jewelry that not only protects you from negativity, but it actively invites positivity into your life as well.

Chapter Summary

- There are many reasons why people use healing crystals in their lives. No one reason is better or worse than another, as these are very personal and determined by the individual's relationship to their crystals.

- We are often controlled by our emotions, but healing crystals are one of the ways we can take control back. By understanding our emotions enough to pick the right crystals to improve them, we get more in touch with ourselves.

- Our chakras often get clogged up and unaligned. This can bring great discomfort to our lives, but these blockages can be cleaned away through the use of healing crystals that help us to align our chakras and live more fully.

- While there are healing crystals for our emotions such as happiness or anger, there are also healing crystals that help us to invite more love into our lives, to connect more fully with those around us, to help us love ourselves, and even to help improve our sexual prowess.

- Certain crystals are said to have properties that improve our psychic powers. We can meditate with them to increase these powers and help us to open up our third eye.

- While some of the benefits of crystals are more ethereal than others, there are those based strongly in science, such as the way that rose quartz, and smoky quartz have been used to improve the health of our skin by being included in beauty products.

- Just because you have a personal relationship with your crystal doesn't mean that your crystal can't also help your plants. Adding the right crystal to the soil around your plants can help to keep them strong and healthy.

- Crystals make up an important part of feng shui, and crystal decorations play a big role in opening up the energy of a room in order to create a much happier and healthier environment that promotes positivity.

- Certain crystals are literally healing crystals in the sense that they can help us to reduce our pain and find relief from the pressures that weigh us down physically, mentally, and spiritually.

- One of the most common uses for healing crystals is to help us to increase the amount of happiness we have in our lives. Some crystals are used to directly enhance our overall sense of joy, while others are used to reduce the amount of depression and anxiety that we experience.

- Practices such as meditation or contemplation with or on our crystals can be a great way to find an island of calm inside that helps us to not overreact to situations, but rather to take events as they come with careful consideration.

- There are also crystals that are used to help remove or prevent negativity energies from overtaking our lives. These crystals are protective and can help us to ward off evil influences that want to ruin our daily lived experience.

In the next chapter, you will learn all about the crystals that help heal our emotions. If you suffer from depression or anxiety, then you can find great relief through the use of the right healing crystals. There are crystals that help to keep us motivated and others that can bring wealth into our lives. There are crystals that help us to experience and find love and others that promote happiness and reduce stress. Regardless of the emotion, there is a healing crystal that will help.

CHAPTER TWO

BEST CRYSTALS TO HEAL YOUR EMOTIONS

Far beyond just our physical health, healing crystals are effective at helping us to heal our emotions, invite positive emotions, and to actualize an abundant lifestyle that encourages us to chase our goals and aim high. If we want to live a life that is as meaningful as possible, as positive as can be, and filled with happiness, love, health, and serenity, then we should seek out the help of crystals. They'll make these goals much easier to achieve.

With that said, the biggest question becomes, "What crystal should I use?" This is another question that isn't easy to answer. The answer is going to be based on what you want your healing crystals to help you with. If you are seeking motivation, then you'll use different stones than you would if you're after love. Anxiety would use different stones, as well. Of course, each of these categories will have a little crossover, but no category will be composed of the same crystals as another. One of the reasons for this is the huge variety of crystals. Happy Glastonbury's list of crystals mentions that there are almost 200 of them, while their A to Z list of crystals has 255 different examples, including the various permutations of each crystal. For an example of this, consider that the site lists apricot, black, blue-banded, blue lace, crazy lace, green, moss, purple, tree, and yellow agates. They're all agates, but a yellow agate is going to have a different energy compared to a purple one.

To get a better sense of the many kinds of crystals, this chapter divides up our emotional and lived spheres so we can look at which crystals are used in matters of love, depression, wealth, or motivation. If you already know the areas that you need an assist, then this can help you to pinpoint which crystals you should begin using. If you aren't yet sure as to what you want healing crystals to help you out with, then this chapter might enable you to get ideas, but you are going to find more useful information in chapter three and our discussion aimed at introducing beginners to their first crystals.

Crystals for Depression and Anxiety

If you have ever suffered from anxiety or depression, then you know exactly how many such issues can ruin your life. They can make it impossible to get out of bed.

They can make you nervous about even leaving the house or picking up the phone. These are debilitating conditions that can feel like a noose wrapped around your neck. When you are facing them, you may feel there is no way to get help. If you are dealing with depression and anxiety, you should seek out educated and certified assistance. However, therapy and other solutions of this ilk aren't performed in a vacuum. You still need to live and go about your life in between your sessions. These periods can feel like drowning in the ocean while waiting for another island to set your feet on (your next therapy session).

Crystals might not be enough to get you out of the ocean of depression, but they can act as a raft, which helps you to navigate the rough waters. They become tools that work alongside the therapy so as to provide you with relief. As you grow stronger and get a better understanding of your depression or anxiety, you may find that you need fewer therapy sessions. Despite this, I am convinced you will find yourself holding onto your crystals as they will continue to help you so long as you let them. So, without further ado, let's take a look at which crystals are the most effective for tackling these dark beasts.

First up is citrine. In specific, you should look for citrine that is closer to being transparent rather than yellow like quartz. A clear citrine of this type will work a lot more effectively for the purposes of helping to alleviate depression. When used for dealing with depression, citrine doesn't add value to your life the same way that crystals for happiness do. Instead, it helps to remove the negative energies surrounding you and causing your depression. If you can find a rarer smoky citrine, then this is even more effective. Smoky citrine is a naturally forming citrine that looks almost like it has cigarette smoke trapped inside, and it can be easy to tell the difference between the two when compared together. This smoky citrine provides the added benefit of helping to lift your mood, while also working to remove the negativity that has infected you.

Another great healing crystal is sunstone. This beautiful looking gem is made up of a mixture of yellowish-orange and pink that immediately makes you think of happier days. There are lots of little sparkles in the stone which allows it to positively glow when the light hits it. This is fitting since sunstone will help to leave you glowing. The light color reflects the way that sunstone helps to lift your mood to invite a more positive, bright energy into your life. As you begin to work with healing crystals, you will likely discover that some are quite heavy. Not in a physical sense, but their energies are too intense for some beginners. Sunstone has a gentle energy that helps to heal, but it doesn't overpower. That makes it a wonderful choice for those dealing with depression and for those who aren't yet experienced in managing the energies of these crystals.

We talked about smoky citrine, but it isn't the only smoky crystal to make the list. In fact, citrine is a kind of quartz, and another great crystal for helping with depression is smoky quartz. This quartz has a very dark color, almost as if the smoke trapped inside had stained the surface. That might sound unappealing, but it is actually quite a beautiful kind of quartz, very different from how we normally think of it. Smoky quartz works similarly to citrine in that it helps to remove the negative energy from your life. The less negative energy around you, the less negativity weighing down your mind and perverting your thoughts. This is a very powerful crystal, though it has a power that isn't overly intrusive.

However, you need to make sure that you cleanse smoky quartz on a regular basis. If it is left to absorb the negative without ever being cleansed, then you will find that it starts to invite more negativity into your life. As long as you purify it on a regular basis, it will continue to help improve your mind and energy. You can find out how to cleanse your healing crystals in chapter five.

Another terrific choice is rose quartz. You might begin to notice a pattern here. Generally speaking, quartz crystals are among the most powerful for dealing with depression and negative mental energies. As this is the case, rose quartz fits in perfectly with citrine and smoky quartz. This type of quartz has a very light pink color that almost borders on white. Instead of removing negative energies, this type of quartz invites in lots of warmth and positive energies, which can help to bring comfort to those facing the turbulent experience that is depression. Rose quartz is also used for helping to reduce stress, and it also promotes a level of self-love that might seem absent when we are depressed. For the most benefit from this powerful crystal, keep it close to your heart in a necklace or even simply by storing it in your breast pocket.

Angel Aura is a type of quartz that has been treated with platinum or silver. This produces a lovely shine. It has an iridescent quality, which is only enhanced by the light, almost pastel colors, that the crystal takes on. This particular quartz crystal can be too powerful for beginners, but those that have the experience to benefit from it can immediately feel the way that it begins to work. Hold it in your hand to feel how it sends vibrations up your arm and deep into your soul. This makes it an effective tool for dealing with a negative mindset. Simply take the angel aura in your hand, close your eyes and focus on it for a few moments. Right away, you will feel how hope starts to return to you. It helps to open up your heart and let you invite in the positive healing energies that are all around us every day.

You might have noticed the way crystals of specific colors help in dealing with negative experiences. Smoky crystals are extremely useful in pulling out negative energy and trapping it, thereby removing it from you, and keeping it in the crystal until you are able to cleanse it. Also common is the way that lighter colored crystals help to bring positive energy into your life. Carnelian is a crystal that is mostly red, but lighter points of white make some parts of it closer to orange or pink. Carnelian is a great crystal for lifting your mood, bringing in positive energy, and reducing the levels of anxiety in your life. It can also help to keep you motivated, making it a versatile healing crystal that could easily fit in several of the categories that we're exploring this chapter.

Crystals for Stress and Anxiety

Stress and anxiety are no laughing matter. They may not

be considered to be quite as bad as clinical depression, but that doesn't mean they can't also deeply impact your life and reduce your level of comfort. If you are dealing with anxiety, then you may want to consider talking to a medical professional about what help is available to you. If you are dealing with high levels of anxiety, then you will want to adopt practices such as meditation or gratitude journaling, both of which are proven to help reduce the levels of cortisol that flow through your body on a daily basis. All of these are positive actions you can take to help the effects of these problems, but they don't need to be the only steps you take. There are lots of healing crystals that will help you in managing these feelings, and you can even combine them into your healthy practices, such as including one of the following crystals into your meditation routine. When it comes to anxiety, stress, and even depression, it is important to use every resource available to you as these issues should never be taken lightly.

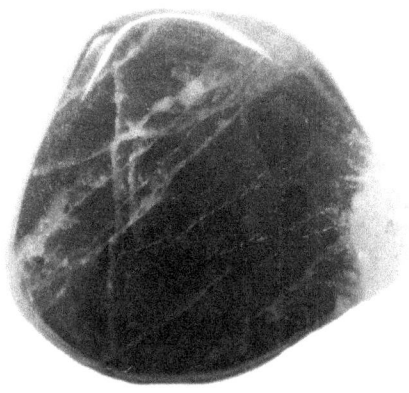

If you're looking to reduce anxiety and stress in your life, perhaps there is no better choice than sodalite. This beautiful blue crystal has been given the nickname, "the stone of peace," and if you have ever dealt with stress, then you know how vital it is to find some peace of mind in the midst of your struggles. This crystal is used to help you achieve this and to reduce the likelihood of panic attacks. This crystal is powerful enough to work even when it is only kept in your pocket, though, ideally, you will want to hold in your hand to let it suffuse through your body. Its blue color is associated with peace, calm, and relaxation. It helps to reduce the overall level of stress you are feeling. Sodalite is also useful in bringing confidence into your life and helping you to express yourself more fully, which makes it a great choice for anyone preparing to give a public speech. Reducing the stress and helping you express yourself is a powerful combination for tackling anxiety and spotlight jitters.

Turning to another blue crystal, we have kyanite. One of the things that can cause a lot of stress and anxiety in your life is when your spiritual nature isn't properly integrated into your life. Losing sight of your spiritual nature can cause you to feel disconnected from the world around you, and it can make you anxious without even knowing it or realizing why. One of the ways we can find our spiritual selves again is through meditation or mindfulness retreats, but these aren't always an option. A quicker and easier way to reach that spiritual self is to practice short meditation sessions using kyanite. This blue crystal is fantastic in helping to connect you to that spiritual level and to realign the chakras in your body to keep them open and flowing fully. If you are dealing with anxiety, stress, fear, anger, or more of those negative feelings, kyanite can help you to release them rather than allow them to stick and fester in your mind. The coolest part of kyanite is the fact that it doesn't absorb these negative emotions the way that a crystal like smoky quartz does. This means that you don't ever need to cleanse kyanite, making it one of the most effective and easy ways to get help dealing with your stress and anxiety.

Moving away from the lighter colored crystals, we find shungite. This dark stone is such a deep blue color that it often appears to be pure black. Shungite is recommended for the way that it helps to protect wearers from electrical-magnetic fields such as those produced by today's plethora of electronics. If you have a lot of stress coming from your workplace, then adding some shungite to your desk will help to bring it down. It is also great for the way it helps to protect you from negative energies that would otherwise bring you down and weigh heavily on your mind. Shungite does need to be purified frequently; otherwise, it will grow less effective until it finally fails to provide any value at all. But if you make it a habit to cleanse it, shungite can be one of the most important crystals in your collection.

In complete contrast of color is Himalayan salt rock. Mostly white, though sometimes pink, Himalayan salt rock is used to help remove negative energy from the body so that you can stay positive and let go of the stress and anxiety that weighs you down. You can find Himalayan salt in the grocery store, though this isn't quite the same. You want to purchase it in rock form rather than ground up. This rock form of the salt is used in salt lamps that create a rainstorm-like effect through electromagnetics. If you purchase Himalayan salt rock for your diet, then it will have some positive influence, but as a healing crystal, you should have some in a vial that you can keep on your person or attached to a necklace. If you have more than you need for this, you can add a little to a bath. Himalayan salt rock is high in vibrations and can turn any bath into a cleansing experience that helps you to literally wash away the worry and anxiety that you're dealing with. When used regularly, this can help you to correct your sleeping schedule and keep you feeling connected to the world around you and your life. These are aspects of existence that we often lose sight of when we are prey to fears and anxiety.

We spoke about rose quartz in the previous section, but it is worth briefly mentioning it again here. Not only is it excellent for helping you to overcome depression, but it can be as effective in tackling anxiety and reducing stress. If it is stress that you are trying to deal with, then rose quartz should be kept in a location where you can readily see it, as it will help to serve as a visual reminder to take care of yourself and relax. For added benefits, put a little Himalayan salt rock into a bath and keep some rose quartz on the side of the tub. These will help to calm you down and remind you to really take part in the bath, to be in the moment with it, and to see it as an opportunity to relax, time that is meant for you.

In the last section, we looked at sunstone, but this time around, we're looking at the reverse: moonstone. This beautiful, milky white stone looks so appealing that you could almost eat it right up. Moonstone has strong ties to motherhood, and it is recommended to keep it on you if you wish to increase your chances of getting pregnant, as well as to keep the pregnancy healthy and to help reduce the pain and discomfort of childbirth. This makes the moonstone far more effective for women than for men. Part of this is the strong connection it has to female hormones, and it can help women to let go of stress and realign their natural intuition with the world around them. If you are feeling lost or worried, hold a piece of moonstone in your hand while you meditate and focus your attention on the healing vibrations that it emits.

Note, men can still use moonstone, of course, but it won't have the same profound connection that it has with women.

The final crystal that we'll look at for stress and anxiety is howlite. While it also happens to be white, it doesn't look much like moonstone at all. Instead, the white of howlite is very bold and dense, and it often has veins of grey or black lines that snake through it to give it a really neat appearance. In fact, one of the best ways of using howlite is to meditate with it while tracing these dark links with a finger. When we are overly worried, we often aren't getting enough sleep, and this only serves to make the issue worse. Place a piece of howlite underneath your pillow to benefit from its soothing energies so that you can get to sleep much easier. Howlite is such a calming crystal that it is often recommended to help teach patience. It is also a crystal that promotes understanding and wisdom, which helps to reduce the struggles you experience in life by removing feelings of anxiety or anger, emotions that can make you lose sight of your spiritual self. While it is most commonly placed under the pillow, you can also keep some in a pocket or add a piece to a bracelet so as to carry the benefits with you throughout the day.

Crystals for Happiness

If you are dealing with depression or anxiety, then it is readily clear how important it is to get help in minimizing the damage of these negative emotions. But we can also approach it from the other side. It might be less apparent that we can make our lives better by increasing the positivity and happiness that we are feeling. We shouldn't only be using crystals in order to remove the bad. They are also amazing tools that let us amplify the positive. It is great to be happy, but it is even better to be ecstatic. You'll notice a couple of the crystals that we look at in this section have been mentioned previously. This is important to note because it helps us to see the way that these crystals don't just work to achieve one result. They can actually help us to achieve several goals at once, such as increasing contentment while also reducing stress. Of course, reducing stress will help us to reach our happiness more readily, and so these goals aren't mutually exclusive in any sense of the word. They're just different paths to the same destination.

Let's start by looking at those crystals which we have already seen. You will remember that quartz is strongly linked to helping remove negativity. Rose quartz is often used for love, but it also helps us to reach into the compassion inside of us. When we can tap into our compassion, we get better at applying it to ourselves, and this lets us practice self-love. Not only does self-love help us to reduce our depression, but it helps us to be more content and happy with who we are and the life that we are living.

Smoky quartz is another that we've seen in regards to depression. This one helps to take negativity out of our lives, but it requires us to cleanse it often so that it keeps working. Along with this, smoky quartz is also good for helping bring a more positive energy into our lives. Part of this is the fact that the negative is removed, but removing the negative doesn't necessarily bring in the positive. Thankfully, smoky quartz also invites rays of positivity to fill up the space where our negativity once was.

Clear quartz also removes negative energy and makes room for positivity. Clear quartz has been called the master healer because it helps not only to remove negativity, but also helps purify body, mind, and soul. This is necessary to open up our chakras and prevent unconscious blockages which prevent us from living our lives with as much joyfulness as possible. We discussed the way that losing sight of our spiritual selves can bring a lot of darkness into our lives and make us feel lost. Clear quartz is one of the most effective crystals we have to enable us to reconnect with our spiritual selves.

Finally, the last of the crystals we have already explored in this chapter is citrine. This crystal has a very free and open energy, which invites us to feel confident and content, a great combination for bringing more happiness to our souls. As with any of these crystals we've seen before, citrine can be used specifically to promote more positivity. What that means is you don't need to reach for these crystals only when there is negativity to be removed. With that understood, let's move on to some new crystals.

Amazonite has a lot in common with citrine in the way that both crystals help to create a more hopeful experience with a free loving attitude. When we try to stop up our love and add barriers to it, we do a great disservice to our happiness. Amazonite helps us to stay authentic, with a heart open up to the world as a whole. This is fantastic because, most of the time, we aren't even aware of the way we have created barriers around our hearts. Amazonite helps to break these down and let us tap into the limitless happiness that is inside of each and every one of us.

Amethyst is another gorgeous crystal, as many of them are. While amethyst helps us to be more positive and happy, it also helps us to stay calm. When we face trouble by panicking or freaking out, we only serve to make our anxiety stronger. But when we face struggles with calmness, we are able to stay closer to our happiness. Struggles no longer take that happiness away from us. We can find the time to look directly at our struggles and see them for what they are. When we do this, we are more readily able to tackle and deal with them without losing our positivity in the process. Keep a piece of amethyst close to your heart to help stay calm and open. That will help us to stay more tightly connected to our spiritual selves, which is always a positive for our soul.

If you are looking for crystals to help with happiness, but you aren't entirely sure which to go with, it is a good bet to stick to the color yellow. These crystals bring to mind the sun and the way the brightness of its rays dispel the darkness of the night. Tiger's eye and yellow jasper are two examples of yellow crystals that serve to prove this point explicitly. Tiger's eye is fantastic for helping us tap into our inner strength and not let our happiness be diminished. Keep a piece of tiger's eye close at hand for any time you need to tap into this strength. It is also useful in helping us to expand our consciousness to see from different perspectives. That makes it excellent for anyone who works in a creative field or one in which they need to generate unique ideas. Yellow jasper, on the other hand, is almost entirely focused on bringing a positive light into our lives. It can help to bring confidence, though we are always more confident when we are happy, and so this could be seen as a reflection of the way it opens us up to the nourishing nature of reality.

Black tourmaline seems to go against everything mentioned in the last paragraph, but this isn't technically true. We might naturally assume that if yellow, light-colored stones bring positivity, then darker stones would bring more downbeat qualities. But black tourmaline is used to remove fear from our lives and to help us keep our heads rather than panic. If you are facing a difficult time, then this crystal should be one of the first that you turn to for assistance. It has the added benefit of helping to bring more physical energy, which is so important when going through a hard situation. Negativity often leaves us feeling weak and exhausted, so black tourmaline works to counter this. To get the most significant benefit to your happiness, combine black tourmaline with one of the other crystals on this list.

The final one we'll look at for happiness is ametrine. This crystal also has a lot in common with citrine, which you might notice from their spelling alone. But, more than the spelling, they share a focus on helping us to stay connected to our spiritual selves while pushing negativity away from us. Ametrine is a gender-neutral crystal that allows us to tap into our male and female energies. We are all composed of energies of both kinds, with men having more male energy and women having more female energy. But, as men or women, we need to be in tune with both of these energies to have a healthy and fulfilling experience throughout life. Ametrine helps us to get in touch with these energies in a positive manner, not favoring one over the other. Hold onto ametrine when you meditate or consider placing it over your heart while lying down.

Crystals for Love

One of the most profound elements that unite human beings is the way that we all want to feel loved. We have a biological urge to find a partner and raise a family, to keep our name going. Even those of us who don't want children still want love. To find a partner that respects you and helps to keep you productive, happy, and healthy has motivated millions of people and thousands upon thousands of stories across film, plays, and television. Yet these days there is a tendency to feel a deep loneliness which seems particular to our 21st-century living. We have websites to help us meet partners, and yet we still find ourselves alone. It can feel like there is no way to get over this, like love doesn't belong in our lives.

This is just ridiculous. Of course, we deserve love. We'll find it, too, so long as we look for it. But that doesn't mean that we can't take some steps to help *it* find *us*. One of the ways we do this is by turning to healing crystals with the properties of love. These can help to remind us that we deserve to be loved. This is great because it gives us a better aura, one that invites love to us. What's more, the right crystal can help to attract that love as strongly as any dating site ever could. We've encountered a couple of these stones, but there are far more left to discover. So if you are looking for some assistance in finding romance, then you should be reaching for one of these amazing crystals.

We've covered rose quartz a couple of times, but it is fantastic for increasing the amount of love in your life, specifically the love that you feel inside your heart. We also discussed moonstone, though not in the context of love. Moonstone has a long tradition as a wedding gift, as it is supposed to bring good luck in love. It is important to gift moonstone to both the bride and the groom, as this goes into older European traditions. It is said that if two people wear moonstone on the night of a full moon, then they will fall in love when the light of the moon reflects off the crystal. Traditions like this exist as one of the ways our ancestors made sense of the healing powers of crystals such as these.

Amber is such a beautiful and vibrant crystal that we named it for its color. You'll note that the orange color ties it closely to tiger's eye and yellow jasper. Like those two crystals, amber can attract a lot of positivity into your life, but it is used more often for love rather than happiness. If you are looking to use amber for its romantic properties, then you will benefit most from wearing it close to your heart, as opening up this chakra will do wonders for your love life. This crystal not only attracts romance and love, but it helps to attract your desires in general, be they happiness, health, wealth, love, or peace. It is also said that amber has protective qualities that help to keep you free from evil influences.

When it comes to love, the color most strongly associated is red. The brighter and bolder the red, the more profoundly this connection pops out. Think about lipstick and hearts, how desire and sexuality are intimately connected to red. Garnet is one of the most stunningly bright red crystals and one that absorbs and pulls in intensely romantic and erotic energies. If you are looking to find love, then wearing garnet is a must. Plus, we know that wearing bold colors like garnet help to make us feel more confident, which in turn further helps us to attract a mate. Garnet is also used in helping to enhance the sexual connection between lovers. To get the most benefits, put a garnet next to the bed or have your partner hold it in their hand as you initiate a lovemaking session.

More pink than red, rhodochrosite is also closely connected to the heart. As it happens, rhodochrosite has been given the expressive title, "The Stone of the Compassionate Heart." With a title like that, it can be no surprise that this gorgeous crystal is amazing for helping your tap into the love all around you. Not only does this help to attract romantic love, but it is also used quite often to help with emotional healing. If you have experienced a painful breakup, rhodochrosite will help you to get over the heightened emotions that come with the territory while also helping you to attract a more fitting and compatible romantic partner. Plus, like garnet, this crystal has been connected to improved sexual relations with your partner. Where garnet is more closely connected to the erotic, rhodochrosite is involved more with intimacy as a whole.

Rose tourmaline has an almost blood-red appearance. This has led to rose tourmaline being connected to vampires in popular culture, but in reality, this red should be thought of in a less sensational, but profound light, as closer to the lifeblood that pumps through your heart. It is this blood that keeps you alive, but it is also this same blood that passes through your heart, and with it comes all of the love that you have ever felt. Rose tourmaline taps into this well of love inside us and helps to open up both the chakras in the heart and those in the head. This helps us to connect our love to our spiritual selves and to feel a connection far deeper than the purely physical. Rose tourmaline helps us to link these two elements of ourselves to create a flow of energy more in tune with the natural ebb and flow of romantic passion.

Yet another wonderful crystal for matters of the heart is red agate, and again, we see just how powerfully linked the color red is to our love and compassion. Everyone would agree that the best marriages are those that bring a sense of stability and security to the lovers while leaving enough room for them to grow and experience the many gifts that life offers. Red agate helps to strengthen all of these, and it should be worn by both lovers rather than just one of them. This stone helps us to open up the root chakra, which is the chakra that allows us to feel at home in our body and connected to the world around us. With this connection comes a more profound sense of being linked to our partners, and the fears of jealousy have a tendency to fade away once lovers begin wearing red agate together. If you aren't in a relationship yet, red agate can help you to feel balanced, but it isn't particularly useful in drawing a romantic partner to you the same way as some of the others we've looked at.

Lapis Lazuli breaks from our pattern of red crystals. This blue crystal is used primarily for calming the soul and keeping us steady and grounded in the face of hardship. But this turns out to be especially useful in matters of the heart as well. We often struggle with jealousy, for example. When we get jealous, we want to fly off the handle and accuse our partner of being dishonest or unfaithful. But the calming aura of lapis lazuli can help us to keep our calm and look at the situation with open eyes. When you do this, you are able to more clearly see the relationship you have with your partner for what it is, and you can see the way that misunderstandings occur. For this reason, it is useful to keep lapis lazuli on you at all times. This powerful crystal is also used to help fix the bridges between you and those around you, bridges that you may have thought you had burned. Furthermore, this amazing crystal helps us to get more in touch with ourselves so that we can understand the ways we unintentionally hurt those around us. What this is useful for is gaining the knowledge necessary to better ourselves and apologize. So powerful is this crystal when it comes to interpersonal relationships, that there is even folklore that posits that giving lapis lazuli as a gift is to make a friendship that will last until the end of time.

Even if it isn't an endless relationship, gifting lapis lazuli to your lover can be a way of deeply bonding.

Our final crystal for matters of love is the opal. This multifaceted crystal is used to draw love towards us, while also helping us to more deeply understand our passions and desires. Keep an opal close at hand, and use it in meditation to help open your heart to the world, and to purge the negativity from your system. By helping you to let go of the unconscious stoppages which prevent you from loving fully, opal can assist you in having a more honest and clear dialogue with your partner (or potential partner). Openness and honesty tend to reward us in spades with love, happiness, and wealth, and so an opal should absolutely be a part of your romantic toolkit if you turn to healing crystals for support with the love you foster in your life.

Crystals for Wealth

Less an emotion and more a desire, wealth is one of the primary motivating factors of human existence. We think of wealth primarily in regard to money and income. This isn't wrong, as these are one definition of wealth. But we should also remember that wealth can be intangible, too. We experience a sense of wealth when we look around and see that we have fostered many meaningful relationships. We feel our wealth when we realize that we have built up a successful career and have gained the respect of our peers. When we speak of an abundance of wealth, money is only one way that manifests itself.

This section will primarily focus on money, but these kinds of wealth are closely related. One of the biggest ways in which we cut ourselves off from wealth is psychological. We convince ourselves that we aren't deserving of it and that it will never come to us. Working with crystals can help us to get over this so that not only do we draw wealth towards us, but we are also able to act on it when it comes into our presence. This combination of attraction, then action, is one of the most powerful and meaningful ways of using crystals that we have. Again, we'll start with a couple of crystals that are familiar to us by this point.

We've seen citrine used for several purposes before, but what we haven't mentioned is its nickname: The Lucky Merchant's Stone. We spoke primarily about natural citrine, and this is actually quite rare. When it comes to dealing with depression, natural citrine is the way to go. But most citrine is created by taking amethyst and using heat to treat it. While you wouldn't want to use this form of citrine for your depression, you can certainly use it for the purposes of attracting wealth. With a title like The Lucky Merchant's Stone, citrine has strong links to financial success. If you are planning a business endeavor, you will want to keep citrine close at hand. One way in which to use crystals for wealth is to create a section of your house, room, or office in which you store and set out your intentions for success and money. Citrine is a great addition to one of these displays as it doesn't just invite wealth to us, but it also reminds us that our wealth is exponentially more valuable when we share it with those around us.

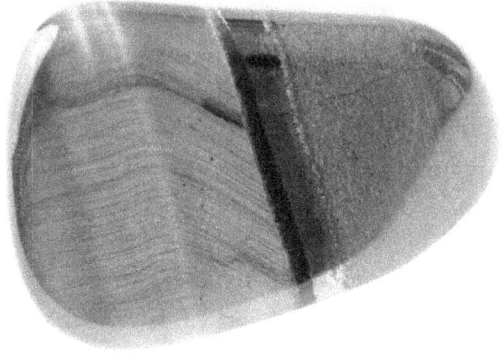

Tiger's eye is another healing crystal that we looked at. Called the stone of the mind, tiger's eye is used to help us to manifest our dreams to bring about a change in our lives. This is not necessarily tied to wealth, as the change we want could be to find love, health, or happiness. But often the change we want most is to find success in our field and to earn enough money to live comfortably. When our dreams are connected to a sense of wealth, that is the time to use tiger's eye to invite reality to meet us halfway. This is important to note, as we can't expect our healing crystals to do all the work. They help us to achieve our goals, but if we never get off the couch to even try to achieve them ourselves, then they will never happen. But so long as you are willing to do the work, tiger's eye will help you to succeed in your actions. If you are starting a new business, protect your wealth, or invite positivity and good fortune into your life, then you should use a piece of tiger's eye. It can be kept on you to help you to prevent wasteful spending when you are out and about, or it can be added to your wealth display to interact with and assist the crystals you are already using.

Quartz is also used to help attract wealth. Specifically, clear quartz crystals. However, to attract wealth, you should only use clear quartz in combination with another crystal. That's because clear quartz can amplify the energy from the crystals around it. So if clear quartz is the only crystal in your wealth display, you aren't going to get any benefits regarding your wealth. It needs something to work on, and there is just nothing for it to help amplify. You will get benefits from it, keep in mind, just not in regard to wealth. Clear quartz is called The Master Healer, and you will get benefits in that regard. But, if you add clear quartz to a wealth display that already has a crystal or two related to attracting wealth, then you will amplify their energies, and make the whole display that much more effective. It should be noted that you can technically infuse clear quartz with any intention, which means that you could use it to attract wealth on its own with enough work and effort on your part, but it is far, far easier to use it for its amplification properties. It is like trying to swim against a river. Technically, you can do it, but it is far more effective if you go with the flow of the river instead.

Next up is fool's gold, otherwise known as pyrite. This stone is amazingly attractive to look at, as it mixes elements of rock with gold to create a glittering appearance that mesmerizes. Any healing crystal of this sort that captures the light to sparkle is a terrific choice for a meditation crystal, as its very appearance helps us to enter into a contemplative state. Hold a piece of pyrite in your hand and focus on it. You can keep it still or move it around in the palm of your hand; either way works. The name fool's gold implies a negative, as nobody wants to be considered a fool. But this name comes to us from the history of trading. People would try to pass off fool's gold as plain old gold. Anyone who fell for this trade was being duped, and was, thus, the fool. But we aren't reaching for pyrite because we think it's gold. We use it because it has a strong force that attracts money. Rather than giving away your fool's gold, keep it close at hand whenever you enter into business situations. It doesn't matter if you are setting up a new business, depositing a cheque, or making an investment, keeping this close at hand invites the universe to look kindly on our transaction so that it will be profitable. We can also use pyrite to help us tap into our courage, as its name comes from the Greek word for fire, and it helps to remind us of the infinite fire of passion that we have inside at any given moment.

One of the key elements we need in order to be successful is luck. It is disappointing to hear that, no matter how well conceived our plans are, no matter how many factors we calculate for, we still need a dose of luck if our plans are to be successful. You might write up a business plan that seems absolutely solid and sound, but then the world can shut down because of an illness. There is too much randomness for us to not rely, to some measure, on luck. But we can improve our luck by using a lucky charm such as a piece of free jade. These crystals have healing properties that can help us to open ourselves up and stop repeating the same mistakes, but they are also fantastic for inviting luck. There is an ancient tradition in China which sees jade as one of the most important substances known to mankind. It was to invoke luck and good fortune that they made jade statues and gave jade as gifts to each other. But the connection of jade and luck goes far beyond Asia and can be seen in cultures as far apart as Russia and Mexico. Jade is especially powerful when used in meditation. It helps us to focus our energy to keep us moving towards our goals. By inviting luck and keeping us going forward, jade brings us much good fortune. Beyond meditation, wearing a jade necklace can let us carry this luck with us throughout our daily lives.

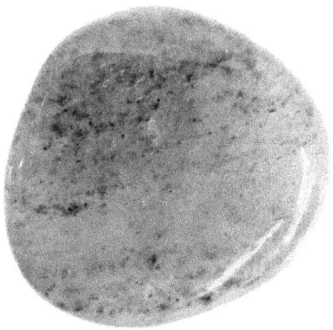

Another gorgeous green stone we can use for attracting wealth is green aventurine. This smooth stone is called the Stone of Opportunity, and if that name doesn't hint at its relationship with attracting wealth, then nothing will. Green aventurine has an intriguing energy that is used to help us regain wealth that we lost due to poorly thought-out plans. Bad investments, wasteful spending, and poor impulse control can all leave us with much less wealth than we are supposed to have. These losses can be devastating and lead us down a path of regret. But what we have lost can come back to us, and green aventurine is foundational in making sure that happens. Green aventurine should be worn in a necklace that hangs over your heart chakra. You may want to wear this throughout the day, but you definitely must wear it while meditating. Some crystals are better served by being held onto during meditation. Green aventurine works best the closer it is to your heart chakra so that its vibrations can help to open it back up and invite abundance into your being.

Love has strong connections to the color red, and happiness is often supported by yellow crystals. You might have figured out already that the color green has a clear link to wealth. Many people seem to think this is due to the fact that paper currency is green, but this only takes into account an American's currency. Yet we see the connection between wealth and the color green in many different cultures. It is more likely that the USA's currency was chosen to be green due to this symbolism and not the other way around. Green aventurine and jade are powerful crystals for attracting wealth, and they are further joined by peridot. Sometimes called the Study Stone, this crystal looks like a green ruby, and the way light passes through it creates an entrancing effect. Peridot is used similarly to clear quartz, in that it can help to boost the energies of the crystals it is used around. More than money itself, peridot is connected to our desires. If you desire love, peridot can help to boost the love-attracting nature of other crystals. If you desire money, then it definitely provides a boost. Add peridot to your wealth display or use it in a crystal grid to get the most benefits. To deeply connect it to wealth, consider creating a grid that uses only green crystals as this level of uniformity can help to make your intentions clearer.

Another green stone we use is the Stone of Hope, Success, and Abundance, otherwise known as amazonite. This stone is very rough, with a turquoise color that is interwoven with webs of white. When you look at it, amazonite seems almost like a piece of the ocean had been captured in a solid form. Not directly tied to money itself, amazonite is used to attract abundance. That might refer to money, but also love, respect, and power could fit into the description. If you are in a position of financial leadership, then amazonite can be a great ally in helping you to stay cool and focused so that you can tackle any issue that arises. Since wealth flows naturally from a successful business, strong leadership is an important and attractive feature to improve through the use of a healing crystal.

Let's close out this section on perhaps the greenest crystal of all. Malachite is sometimes called the Stone of Transformation, and this is seen in the way that the colors shift from light green to dark green and all the shades in between. While jade is a dark green, malachite is a mixture of dark and light green, which makes each shade stand out more clearly through contrast. Malachite is used in removing negativity, making it a healing crystal that you may want to include in grids meant for tackling depression. But the most significant feature of malachite is the way that it attracts energy to it. Not just wealth, but energy itself. This can be the energy or abundance or positive energy that brings happiness and calm. Another name for malachite was the Stone for

Merchants, which more readily links it to wealth. For the best results using malachite, you may choose to keep it in a grid or a display, but it offers the most support when it is kept in your purse or wallet. Our wallets are most readily associated with wealth, and so by having a piece of malachite there, we invite abundance in that specific direction and form.

Crystals for Courage and Motivation

We could all use a little more courage in our lives. Sometimes our bravery is blocked due to depression or anxiety, but often we don't have the ability to access our courage even when we are feeling happy and successful. This is extremely frustrating because each one of us has courage inside. This reservoir is connected to our motivation in a symbiotic relationship. When we have motivation, we need our courage to act on it, and when we can tap into our courage, it becomes easier to keep ourselves motivated. But motivation and bravery often don't come to us as effortlessly as we might like. Sometimes we need assistance. This can come in the form of a spiritual practice like meditation or classes from a life coach or mentor. But these are just some of the more popular ways to access these qualities. One that is simple and surprisingly effective is, you guessed it, healing crystals.

One of the powerful attributes of healing crystals is the

way they give back what you put in. For example, when you turn to a crystal for help in your love life, you get back energy that helps you to attract love and abundance into your life. Choosing crystals with strong ties to the heart helps to increase this return, but you can get benefits even when using the wrong ones. Again, the metaphor of swimming against the current works perfectly here. If we want to get the most benefit to our courage, we should select crystals that help to keep us motivated and feeling brave. However, it is important to consider what you want the courage for. If it is to find financial success, then you should first turn to crystals that invite wealth. If it is for love, then turn to the crystals we looked at in that section. Use the crystals for courage to help amplify and supplement those that are specific to your goals. This will help you to get the most direct benefits for what you desire. It is like seeing a specialist instead of a general practitioner; the results will be much more specific to your needs.

Carnelian is a great choice for motivation, especially if you are looking for motivation to start a new business venture or to keep pushing through a hard time. We often come up against challenges in our lives, and when this happens, it can be easy to retreat and shrink away. To face a challenge is to face a hardship, something that pushes us to grow and be more than we were. We all have this capacity for growth, but we often convince ourselves that we don't. We like to tell ourselves that we are less than we are, and this is a terribly poisonous attitude that can greatly damage our chances of success. If you are having a hard time staying motivated and tapping into your courage, carnelian should be a go-to crystal for you. This crystal helps us to open up our sacral chakra and tap into the unlimited creativity inside of us. It enables us to come up with unique solutions to the challenges we face. One of the biggest things that takes motivation away from us is when we convince ourselves that there is only one answer to a problem and that it isn't a good one. Carnelian helps us to see that there are many solutions to every problem, and with a little bit of consideration and courage, we can discover the way that is right for us.

Despite its bright red color, ruby isn't associated with love like many of the red crystals. Instead, this beautiful stone is associated with nobility and a sense of pride. Its strong vibrational energy helps us to stay rejuvenated so that we can stick it out through even the hardest challenges. This energy can be fantastic for more than just facing obstacles, though. Consider meditating with ruby in the morning so that you can meet each day with more natural energy than normal. One of the factors that drain away our motivation and courage is a lack of energy, and so this helps to cut out the fatigue and keep us meeting each day with robust confidence and a sense of opportunity.

Blue apatite is linked to inspiration. Inspiration itself is tightly linked to motivation. If you've ever had a burst of inspiration, then you know the motivating energy that follows. When inspiration hits, it suddenly feels like nothing else matters, that the only important thing in the world is to act on the inspiration. We might not even consider this feeling to be a sense of motivation because it is so tightly linked to the inspiration. But inspiration provokes motivation, as inspiration itself is not an action or a replicable experience. We can be hit by inspiration when looking at a painting or a cloud, but then the next painting or next cloud won't trigger a thing in our souls. We need inspiration to push us to motivation, but then we need that motivation to carry us through to our next actions. As inspiration fades, it requires more courage to keep going. This holy trinity can benefit from the use of blue apatite to increase the likelihood that inspiration will strike, while also helping us to stay concentrated on our goals. Focus itself is an element of motivation, as we want to push ourselves harder and further when we are focused, and thus we are actually using motivation without realizing it. Blue apatite is such a powerful crystal because of the way it helps us tap into this motivation in a subtle but profound way.

We saw that yellow jasper could help us to tap into a deeper sense of happiness and bring positivity to our lives. That's far from the only purpose that jasper serves, though it is the primary purpose of yellow jasper. If we are looking for help staying motivated and confident, we may want to use yellow jasper, but red jasper is more potent for achieving our purpose. This bright crystal is powerful yet gentle, with an aura that doesn't demand much from the person wearing it. In especially stressful times, we can find ourselves losing our motivation. While you should turn to a healing crystal with stress relief properties, these won't necessarily bring back your motivation. Consider your body as a house for your energy. When you are motivated, your motivation is renting the house. But then comes stress to evict your motivation and take over. You might evict stress by using a healing crystal for stress relief, but this doesn't immediately bring motivation back as a tenant. You need to extend an invitation and coax it back in, and red jasper is one of the most effective tools for achieving this.

On a personal level, this is my favorite crystal. Almandine garnet is among the most beautiful substances on this planet. While it has some of the red that we associate with garnet, it also has hints of blue and green, white and black, yellow, and teal. In a lot of ways, that helps to give it a very intense aura. Unfortunately, this means this particular healing crystal can be too powerful for many people. It has elements of each of the categories that we've looked at, from wealth to love, to motivation and happiness. But almandine garnet can also bring with it some pain. This crystal has a way of making us look deeply at ourselves to see who we are. When we are living a life that doesn't align with our true selves, we are going to find ourselves experiencing pain and disappointment. This has stopped many people from using almandine garnet more than once, but it should be seen, not as a negative, but as a neutral. We wouldn't be upset with what was revealed if we lived our lives according to that deepest, truest version of ourselves. Using almandine garnet may make you feel disappointed, but if you take those lessons and act on them, then each subsequent session with almandine garnet will be much better. While this may not seem directly tied to courage or motivation, consider the way it helps encourage us to live as authentic a life as possible. The closer we get to that true self, the more courage we find in our actions and the fewer doubts we carry with us. Perhaps it is a roundabout way of getting to courage and motivation, but one that will pay dividends for the rest of your life when approached with the correct attitude.

Our final crystal for this section and this chapter is orange calcite. Sometimes called the Stone for Creativity, this crystal looks like a tangerine was turned into a stone. It comes to us exclusively from Mexico, making it one of the more rare crystals to get your hands on. Yet it has an aura that absolutely buzzes with motivation and a sense of unlimited potential. To hold a piece of orange calcite in your hand is to feel a connection to the power inside us. This crystal is primarily used to help promote creativity. It is highly recommended for artists, writers, filmmakers, and anyone else that works in a creative field, or who considers themselves to be an artist regardless of medium. Orange calcite also has amplification properties that will help to increase the effectiveness of the crystals it is used in conjunction with. If you are looking to tap into your motivation and keep going, then perform a lying down meditation, and place the orange calcite on your stomach just above your groin. This will keep it close to the sacral chakra and help to keep it open. If you have the option, adding a piece of orange calcite to your belt will allow you to keep it close to the sacral chakra throughout the day so that you can carry the benefits with you rather than having to take the time to tap into them in the morning or evening.

Chapter Summary

- The most common use for healing crystals is to help us to remove negativity, invite positivity, and take control of our feelings.

- There are more than two hundred different types of crystals, which each has unique properties that we can benefit from.

- Anxiety and depression are crippling afflictions that can suck the joy out of life. While they should never be taken lightly, we can find help dealing with them through our crystals.

- Citrine is a powerful crystal that helps to remove negative energies from around us.

- Sunstone is a yellow and pink crystal that removes negativity and invites positivity.

- Smoky quartz crystals are very potent because they not only remove negativity, but they trap it inside of themselves. This requires them to be cleansed frequently, but it can do wonders for your mental health.

- Rose quartz is most strongly associated with love, but that love is also a sense of self-love, which is something we need in order to feel like we belong.

- Angel Aura is another type of quartz, though it has been treated with a metal to take on an iridescent quality. This is a very powerful crystal that beginners might want to avoid, but it can certainly help to ward off a negative mindset.

- Crystals with a common color tend to offer similar benefits. Yellow is associated with happiness, blue with relaxation, red and pink with love.

- Sodalite is a blue crystal that is so good at helping us to relax that it has been nicknamed the stone of peace.

- Kyanite is another blue and relaxing stone that can help you to feel more connected on a spiritual level.

- Shungite is a dark stone, but it helps to remove negative energies and can block EMF fields.

- Himalayan salt rock might sound more tasty than helpful, but it is high in vibrations and helps to burn away stress.

- Crystals for happiness include smoky quartz, as it removes negativity; rose quartz, for the self love promoting qualities; clear quartz, because it removes negativity and amplifies other crystals; citrine, which helps us to feel confident; amazonite, which works like citrine; amethyst, which promotes a sense of calm in the face of negativity.

- Crystals for love are most often pink or red, such as rose quartz, amber, garnet, rhodochrosite, rose tourmaline, and red agate.

- Lapis lazuli is also a profound crystal for attracting love, despite its blue appearance. This is true for opal as well.

- Crystals that attract wealth are often green. But we also see yellow crystals like citrine or tiger's eye are used for bringing wealth to us.

- Courage and motivation are necessary qualities if we want to live as fully as possible, yet sometimes they can feel like they are in short supply. Carnelian, ruby, blue apatite, yellow jasper, almandine garnet, and orange calcite are powerful crystals that can help you to find the motivation to keep going and achieve your hopes and dreams.

In the next chapter, you will learn about the crystals that are recommended for beginners. While anyone could grab a crystal and start from there, it is best to begin small and work your way up so that you have a sense of how each of these crystals functions and brings about an improvement in your life, your emotions, or your mental experience.

CHAPTER THREE

RECOMMENDED CRYSTALS FOR BEGINNERS

In the last chapter, while looking at crystals for healing specific emotions, we discussed how certain crystals weren't appropriate for beginners. Each crystal has a vibrational force that works to attract different energies to our lives. Sometimes these energies are positive and help to heal us from the detrimental effects of negativity. Other times these energies are used to open us up to creativity, wealth, love, passion, relaxation, motivation, and more. It should immediately be clear why we would want to bring these energies into our lives, but it is helpful to do it in a way in which you don't overwhelm yourself. This might be a little bit confusing to understand, so let's turn to a metaphor.

Ninety percent of the adult population in North America drinks coffee, so let's use this as a jumping-off point. If you prefer, pretend that we are talking about alcohol or beer, as these follow the same pattern as coffee. When you first are introduced to this delicious beverage, it can be quite overwhelming. A single cup can keep you up all hours of the night, and you may even experience muscle spasms. If you haven't had any coffee before, then you absolutely don't want to start with an espresso. But, if you have been drinking coffee for any length of time, then you know how quickly you get used to it. Then you can start drinking extra-strong or even espresso if you want. It will still have a much stronger kick than a regular cup of coffee, but it won't knock your socks off anymore. This is pretty much exactly what happens when we start using crystals. Those that are too powerful can be overwhelming and put us off of using crystals, just like an espresso taken early can make us not want to try coffee ever again. When you build up naturally, you increase your ability to handle the energies of even the strongest crystals.

In order to ensure that you don't jump in at the deep end, this chapter will briefly look at which crystals have an energy that isn't too intrusive for a beginner. You may want to go ahead and grab yourself a strong crystal such as almandine garnet, but you will find your experience to be far more pleasant if you take your time and build up your skill. It is better to build slowly than to burn out quickly, after all!

Hematite

Hematite is used to promote a sense of stability within our emotions. Instead of being all over the place, with our emotions scattered to the winds, hematite helps us to find an island inside ourselves from which we can identify and witness our emotions. From this place, we are able to take much needed calming breaths that help us to remove negativity from our lives. Things like stress and anxiety can be let go of, and the hematite will trap them inside of itself, preventing them from returning to you.

The relaxation that hematite offers makes it a wonderful stone for those who feel like they are often under a lot of pressure. If you are a university student or someone working in a hectic industry, a piece of hematite should be kept nearby to remind you that you are more than your studies or your job. Even though there may be inevitable stresses, they shouldn't be allowed to ruin your mental and spiritual health.

Hematite has a gentle aura, which is ideal for beginners, as it creates a soothing feeling rather than a strong or overpowering one. It needs to be purified regularly to remove the toxic and negative energies that it absorbs. I believe that beginners should always have at least one crystal that requires them to perform a cleansing, as this is a crucial process and should be learned early. Many of the more advanced crystals that you will come to use need to be cleansed quite often, otherwise they can actually backfire and invite more negativity than they remove. Starting with a gentle stone like hematite will allow you to get used to cleansing without increasing the stakes in a large way. The more you can learn at this point, the better off you will be in the long run.

Citrine

We've seen citrine pop up several times throughout this book, and so it should be clear that this is one crystal that is extremely flexible in its uses. It can help you to stay motivated, it can help you to stay positive, it removes negative energy from your life, and it is even used to help attract wealth. Not only that, but it also has connections to fertility and creativity. With all of these disparate features, you might think that this crystal would be overly powerful.

And yet citrine is anything but. While it has an extensive range of possible uses and attracts lots of different energies, citrine is a very mild crystal with a subtle vibrational energy that makes it easy to use. If you could only select one crystal to begin with, you would be well advised to go with a piece of citrine.

Blue Lace Agate

We've looked at red agate, but, really, if you are going to begin with any type of agate, then it should be one of the blue lace variety. This crystal has a smooth texture and a light blue color that helps to promote a sense of calm. We've discussed the way that losing sight of your deeper, truest self can cause a lot of discomfort in life. Blue lace agate is one of the crystals for beginners that is great at helping to heal this divide and reconnect us to that self deep inside. Blue lace agate is used to help us to speak more openly and sincerely, both to ourselves and in our interactions with others.

Blue lace agate is among the best crystals to wear in a necklace, as it is usually strongly tied to the chakra in our throat that helps facilitate communication. If you are in a position in which you need to be a leader, or perhaps even just a public speaker, then a piece of blue lace agate worn around the neck can help to keep you speaking clearly and expressing nothing but your deepest truth.

Clear Quartz

Among the many quartz crystals that we use for healing purposes, clear quartz is one of the strongest and yet also one of the best for beginners. Called the Master Healer, clear quartz is used to help us repair the damage from negativity, keep our aura clear from darkness, release negative emotions which have caused us pain, and even more. It is also one of the crystals which absorb negativity into itself so that it can't re-enter your life. What that means is you will need to learn to practice cleansing rituals so as to keep your clear quartz working at the highest level possible.

Clear quartz also acts as an amplifier. While it doesn't have a strong energy of its own, or, rather, an intrusive energy, clear quartz helps to boost the vibrations of the crystals around it. If used in a spread or a ritual, this can cause another weaker crystal to become much stronger. This is something that beginners need to be aware of. You may be using blue lace agate, for example, because it has a subtle power which makes it terrific for beginners, only to find that it becomes much more difficult to use once clear quartz is introduced. To address this, begin by using clear quartz on its own, and then slowly introduce other crystals into your practice, whether that be meditation, wearing crystal jewelry, or creating a crystal grid. It is always best to build up and introduce new crystals one at a time so that you can feel the difference and not overwhelm yourself in the process.

Amethyst

When you are feeling swamped by life, it is crucial that the crystal you use to help relax and ground you isn't itself overwhelming. This would only exacerbate the problem rather than help to solve it. Thankfully, amethyst is one of the best crystals for clearing the mind, plus one that is a great choice for beginners because of the gentle vibrations it emits. Amethyst also has protective properties that it uses to ward off negative energy that would otherwise seek to keep you down.

Meditation with amethyst will clear the mind and help

boost our spiritual defenses. It can also be used in a grid, though it is important not to add too many crystals to a grid at once when you are beginning. Perhaps the most beneficial aspect of amethyst is the way that it helps to protect us in our sleep. Negative energies often try to get at us through our subconscious, and we see this manifest itself as nightmares. These can prevent us from getting refreshing sleep or even sometimes wake us up in the middle of the night. To prevent these negative energies from disturbing our rest, place a piece of amethyst under your pillow before bed so that you can benefit from the protection it offers.

Pyrite

Known as fool's gold, pyrite is used to promote wealth and success in business. Keeping a piece of pyrite at your workspace can help you to achieve more, get a promotion, and invite healthy energy into the workspace, a place which may typically have a problem with attracting positivity. Another of the benefits that pyrite offers is a deep sense of confidence, which is fantastic for those that need to assert themselves in their jobs.

Where some crystals have a strong energy that can be overwhelming, pyrite has a strong energy that helps to improve your willpower. If you are finding yourself unable to get motivated or to push through work and deal with the other tasks you have on your plate, meditating with pyrite and keeping it nearby will help you to overcome these challenges.

Chapter Summary

- Despite the fact that all of the crystals we have discussed bring a positive force, these energies can be overwhelming if you aren't yet used to them.

- It is best to start with some crystals that have a more subtle vibration so that you can get used to them and build up your tolerance. You should also try starting with only one crystal at a time, getting used to it, and then moving onto another. In time, you can build up your skills to be able to deal with the energy from thousands of crystals at once.

- Hematite is a crystal that helps us find stability in our emotions, to relax when things are getting scary, and to remember that we aren't the situations we find ourselves in. Hematite has a gentle aura, though it works to amplify the crystals around it, so you should use it with caution.

- Citrine is a crystal for many purposes. Despite the fact that it can be used for so many different things, it has a very peaceful and subtle energy which makes it great for beginners. If you can only get one crystal to begin, get a citrine.

- Blue lace agate has a smooth texture and light blue color that help it to increase the sense of calm you feel when holding onto it. It is also used to help us speak more honestly, and so it benefits from being worn as a necklace so it can be close to the throat chakra.

- Clear quartz is a powerful crystal, often called the master healer because of the way it helps to heal our body, mind, and soul. The powerful aura that clear quartz has is great for helping us to get over the damage caused by negativity. It's important to note that clear quartz acts as an amplifier to increase the power of crystals nearby. This can make a subtle crystal turn into an overwhelming crystal, so use carefully.

- Amethyst is a fantastic crystal for relaxing and clearing your mind. It has protective properties and stops negative energy from getting you down. Beginners should try sleeping with a piece of amethyst under their pillow to ward off bad dreams.

- Pyrite, also known as fool's good, helps us succeed in business and find wealth. Of the crystals related to wealth, it is the most approachable for beginners who should consider keeping a piece near their workspace to benefit from the deep sense of confidence it provides.

In the next chapter, you will learn how to use your

crystals. There are many different ways in which we can use them, but we'll be sticking with the most typical, as these easily make up 80% of how most people will want to employ them. The most common approach is to wear your crystals as jewelry, but their uses can differ widely. Some use their crystals for home decor, others sleep with them to get their benefits, while they're unconscious, and others meditate with their crystals, or use them in various rituals. When it comes to using them, always follow your heart and intuition. The crystals themselves will generally provide a guide to what's right for you.

CHAPTER FOUR

HOW TO USE HEALING CRYSTALS

While looking at individual crystals, we have discussed some of the ways in which they are best used. These have mostly covered meditation or wearing them as jewelry. These are certainly the two most common ways to use crystals, and as such, they will each be discussed in this chapter, but they are far from being the only ways. We'll be looking at how we can use crystals in ways ranging from meditation to bathing, drinking to sleeping, and from gardening to jewelry. We'll even make a few more stops between each of these, as there really are just so many different methods for you to utilize your crystals.

If you are unsure of what the best approach is, then you should start simple with meditation or jewelry. Both of these methods can significantly improve your life as you tap into the energy inside of your crystals, and, in time, they will help you to grow comfortable enough to branch out and experiment with other applications. All the variations that you find in this book are potent, and there isn't a single method that is right or wrong. It all depends on what is best for you, and only you have the power to make that decision. When dealing with energies such as these, your intuition and gut-feeling are more important than anything I could ever tell you. With that said, let's look at the many ways in which people have put these amazing tools to use.

Meditation

Among all of the ways of using your crystals, meditation is by far the most powerful. This is because meditation itself is a powerful tool. Often considered as part of the Buddhist belief system, meditation doesn't have to be necessarily thought of as a religious or spiritual practice. For many people, it can be a way of getting in touch with their spiritual self, but just as many others meditate because science has shown that it is one of the most beneficial practices for health. It helps us to calm down, reduce our stress levels, boost our happiness, and increase our life expectancy. All of these bonuses come when we meditate, whether we're using a crystal or not. But if we add a crystal to our meditation and use it as our point of focus, we are able to achieve much more out of this practice. If you haven't meditated before, don't worry. It isn't that hard, and adding a crystal to your practice is very simple.

Let's begin by looking at meditation itself. There is a misconception that meditation is the act of sitting down and clearing our minds. This may happen when we meditate, but it isn't actually how meditation works. That's important to remember because I have encountered many people who say they can't meditate because their minds are too active. Ironically, by saying that they are putting the finger on their problem. It is exactly these people who need meditation the most. When we meditate, we often do manage to clear our minds, but this is a byproduct of meditation rather than meditation itself. Plus, when we practice meditation properly, we increase our ability to clear our minds and focus on a single thing at a time. This helps to improve how well we focus on the other elements in our lives, such as the work we have on hand.

To meditate, find somewhere comfortable to sit or lie down. Some practices, especially Buddhist practices, are very specific about the posture of the body during meditation. If you are just starting, don't worry too much about this. Just find a position that is comfortable for you to stay in for ten minutes. Close your eyes and take a deep breath through your nose. Hold it for five to seven seconds, then slowly let it go out of your mouth. Repeat this. That is all basic meditation is. People think that they are supposed to sit down and clear their minds, but this isn't the case. All you need to do is focus on your breathing. You may find that your mind begins to wander, and you might even consider this to mean you have failed. But as soon as you realize that your attention has wandered, you bring it back to your breathing. It is through the act of bringing your attention back to your breathing that you make it easier to focus further down the road. It can seem counter-intuitive, having to lose your focus in order to develop it, but this is the same thing that happens when we are learning new information. When we try to remember something, we often think that having a hard time remembering it is a bad sign. But if you are learning a new topic, it is the act of struggling to remember that makes it easier. By going through our minds to find the information, we make the information take a stronger hold. Thus, by losing our focus and then returning it, we make it easier for us to keep our focus in the future.

So, as a general guideline, that is how you meditate. Now, let's add a crystal to the practice.

Rather than focusing on your breathing, when meditating with a crystal, you focus on the crystal. This is easiest done when you focus on the physical feeling of the crystal. For example, some people like to lie down and place a crystal on their forehead. This practice is primarily used to strengthen your third eye or psychic tendencies. Another way is to hold your crystal in your hand, or even to hold a different crystal in each hand. Rub your thumb over the crystal and really concentrate on the way that it feels. You shouldn't have to open your eyes this way, although you can if you want to. Opening your eyes when meditating isn't recommended because the visual senses can easily break you out of your concentration. When meditating traditionally, we focus on the feeling on the rise and fall of the chest and the cold, crisp feeling of the oxygen as it fills our lungs. When we meditate with a crystal, we replace this feeling with that of the crystal itself. It is important to have this physical feeling because it is through focusing on this that the brain begins to quiet down the regions not necessary to maintain the focus. It is this act of quieting that people think is meditation itself, not just the result thereof.

When we meditate with a crystal, we carefully select the crystal we are going to use based on the attributes that we are looking to invite into our lives. If we are looking for love, then we would meditate with a rose tourmaline or another love-focused crystal. For wealth, we might meditate with a piece of jade. Rather than focusing on the crystal's intentions, we focus on the physical aspect of the crystal and let the intention naturally come out and fill us up. When we try to focus too much on the intention, we get lost in our minds as we consider things like the reason we choose that intention. The reason isn't crucial; what is important is narrowing your focus and opening yourself up as widely as possible. This can't happen when we're running through our minds and unintentionally bringing in extraneous emotions to the session. You may want to take a few minutes prior to meditation to focus on the intention, but once you are meditating, all of that needs to be let go of and set aside until after you have finished.

Meditation is best done once or twice a day. It is recommended to meditate in the morning before the day gets fully started. Doing this is great for our mental health, but it is even better when meditating with crystals as it allows us to tap into their energies before anything happens in the day. The longer we wait, the more issues we risk encountering. For example, if you go about your day and continue to get stressed out, then you will probably turn to meditation with a relaxing crystal. But if you begin the day by meditating with a calming crystal, you are far less likely to let that would-be stress affect you in the first place. Starting early is always recommended. Likewise, it is also recommended that you pay attention to getting restful sleep at night. While you are unconscious, your brain is still pumping away and living. It uses this time to make sense of the day and to defuse harmful energies. If we are bringing negative energies with us to sleep, then they can make this experience lousy, filled with nightmares or tossing and turning. But a meditation before bed helps to protect ourselves from these energies and invite more positivity into the experience. Meditating twice a day might seem like a lot, but it's only 20 minutes, far less time than we waste checking social media or scrolling through the channels of the TV. Plus, if you are tight on time, it is good to know that as little as two minutes a day can have a positive effect on your life. You can also set the intentions for your crystals before getting home or while you are in the shower so that you can jump right into the meditation without wasting any time.

Carrying Crystals

The easiest way to use your crystals is to carry them with you throughout your day. This might seem too easy, but it can have a surprisingly powerful effect. To get the most out of our crystals, we need to attune to them and develop a relationship with them. When you first buy a crystal, it will bring in energy to your life, but it is kind of like trying to fit a square peg in a round hole. You might get some of the potency out of it, but there is a lot more that isn't helping you yet. But as you spend more time with your crystals, you start to create a much better fit. It's as though the edges of that square peg have been worn down so that now it's a round peg that fits perfectly into a round hole. We aren't literally wearing away any part of us or our crystals, but the metaphor gets the idea across.

You can toss a crystal into a purse and still get some benefit, but it is better to keep it closer to yourself. A breast pocket is the best, but the pocket in your pants is also a good fit. If you are using a crystal that is associated with the heart chakra, then you should use the breast pocket or consider wearing a necklace that allows the crystal to hang over your heart. You can still put one of these crystals into a pants pocket, but it won't be as effective. Crystals associated with the sacral chakra are better off in your pants compared to around your neck, so it is all about putting the specific crystal as close as possible to the chakra it's intended to open.

With that said, if you don't have a way to keep a heart chakra crystal near your heart, then don't feel like there is any reason not to take it with you in a pocket. It is far better to have it on your person rather than leaving it at home. This is especially true if you are heading out to face a tough experience or one that causes you nervousness. You can always reach into your pocket to feel the crystal and tap into its positive energies for courage, strength, or whatever you are looking to gain from it.

Drinking a Crystal Elixir

Out of all the possible ways of using crystals, this is the one that could hurt you the most. Before we even get into how to make a crystal elixir, we need to talk about the possible risks. There are some crystals that are toxic when consumed. For example, amazonite is poisonous and could cause a lot of bodily harm if ingested.

Furthermore, there are crystals such as celestite, which can break apart or degrade when put into liquid. Before making a crystal elixir, you should always take the time to open up Google and search, "Is [crystal] safe for use in an elixir?" That will give you an idea if there are any health concerns you need to be aware of. Make sure you consult with reliable and reputable sources before proceeding with your elixir. With that said, we'll look now at what a crystal elixir is, how to make one, and how we can make one with a toxic crystal without in any way risking our health.

A crystal elixir is one of the ways we can get as close as possible to our crystals and the energies that they contain. Rather than keeping those energies outside of ourselves and requiring them to pass through our bodies from the outside in, we can infuse water with crystal so that we can literally ingest the energy from the crystal so that it fills up our bodies from the inside. This process can be quite powerful, and beginners should start with one of the crystals recommended in chapter three, and only after they've spent time getting used to that crystal's particular vibrations. However, if you believe that you are in control of your relationship with your crystal, and not likely to be overwhelmed, then making a crystal elixir can be like making crystal energy drinks. Instead of caffeine and wakefulness, you create a drink which helps to fill you up with the positive properties of your chosen crystal.

To begin with, you need to cleanse it. Even if you have just purchased a new one for yourself, you should cleanse it before using it anyway, let alone using it to make a crystal elixir. We'll cover cleansing in the next chapter. For now, let us assume that you have properly cleansed the crystal you are looking to use in your elixir. The next step is to fill a container up with fresh water. This is best done with spring water that doesn't have any chemicals added to it for cleaning purposes. If you have access to well water, then this will work, but it's advisable to avoid using tap water, as you can't be sure what is in it. Next, place your crystal into the water. There are two camps as to what to do now. One camp sees this as the point in which you drink the water, with the crystal still in it. But the other viewpoint, which I recommend, suggests leaving the crystal in the water overnight to soak. In the morning, you can remove the crystal and choose to drink the elixir then. Or you can store it in the fridge to make it last longer. I like to mix up a big batch in a juice pitcher so that I can fill my water bottle several times. I also tend to have two pitchers of crystal elixir or more in my fridge at a time so that I can choose the right type of drink to help me with whatever it is I happen to be going through that day.

As mentioned above, not every crystal is fit for making a crystal elixir this way. Those that would cause us harm should not be ingested in any way. But this doesn't mean that we can make elixirs using them, just that we have to be careful. If you want to make a crystal elixir using a crystal like amazonite, you should get yourself a container with a top like a mason jar. Fill the jar up with water and then put the top on. Sit the crystal on top of the lid and keep it there overnight. In the morning, you have yourself a crystal elixir without any risk of causing harm. This elixir won't be as powerful as one that can soak directly, but it is still quite effective.

You should note that there are water bottles that you can buy, which are designed to have a crystal placed in them. These are often quite expensive, though they are very beautiful, and they make it easy to create a crystal elixir. But in no way should you feel like you have to invest in one of these. You could make a crystal elixir in a mason jar, a juice jug, or even a pot of water if it was all you had. Just make sure that you use cleansed crystals and, when using toxic crystals, make sure they have no direct contact with the water you're drinking.

Bathing

One of the best ways to use relaxing crystals is to add them to your bath. Just like with crystal elixirs, you should be careful not to add toxic crystals into your bath water as these toxins can be absorbed through the skin and cause lots of damage to your body. You should also avoid using crystals like pyrite as pyrite turns into sulfuric acid when combined with water, and I can't think of anything less relaxing than an acid bath! But, so long as the crystal is safe to add to water, then you may want to place it directly into the bath. Those crystals which can't be added to the bath can be kept on the ledge of the tub or nearby so as to offer their energy to the room.

Bathrooms are often the smallest rooms we have in our houses, so keep in mind how tight the space is when you are preparing for a crystal bath. The more crystals you bring into the space, the more energy you are bringing in, and this can quickly become overwhelming. Taking a bath is one of the worst places to have a feeling of being overwhelmed. The bath is so comfortable you don't feel like getting out to move the crystals, but the overwhelming feeling prevents us from fully enjoying ourselves. Nothing is more disappointing than getting out of the bath and feeling as tight and wound up as we did when we first sat down.

If you are mindful of what crystals you use and what energy they bring, then taking a crystal bath can be one of the more relaxing experiences of your life. Consider bringing in crystals on the blue spectrum, as these tend to have the most calming vibrations. Of course, you don't necessarily need to take a bath to soothe yourself. It can be an intimate and bonding experience to bathe with a lover, and a bath of this sort could benefit from red, love-oriented crystals rather than those with an aura of relaxation. A bath can also be a fantastic way to meditate, so you may want to bring in crystals to promote wealth, health, happiness, motivation, or more.

Keep in mind the way that the various energies change the feeling of the bath. Start with only one crystal at a time until you are comfortable enough to bring in several as you relax in the water.

Crystal Grid

Creating a crystal grid is one form of ritual that we can perform with our crystals. As such, it's helpful that you stick to what you feel inside when working with them. There are some suggestions that you can find online for how to make a crystal grid, such as arranging your crystals in a circular pattern, but if you want to amplify the energy of your crystals as much as possible, then you should follow your instincts and arrange them as you see fit.

CRYSTALS FOR BEGINNERS

To perform a crystal grid ritual, you must start with an end goal in mind. This initial step is something that we will be looking at more in detail in the next chapter. For now, take a moment to figure out what it is you want. Perhaps you are trying to let go of some unhappiness or anger. Maybe you are trying to attract romantic love into your life. Whatever the reason that drives you, make sure that you understand it and have it mind when you start. Next, select crystals that have an energy that supports this desire. How many crystals you choose is up to you; just remember that beginners should start with fewer crystals and slowly work their way up by adding a new one only after getting used to the energy of those they're working with. It can be easy to blow out and create a negative feeling when we are inundated with the power of our crystals.

Once you have selected those crystals which will make up your grid, start to arrange them in front of you. You can place them however you like, based on a pattern that you've seen before or simply place them where it feels right. When you are starting, the chances are that you will be placing the crystals on this instinctual basis, and that will be all the meaning that each placement holds. But as you work more often with crystal grids, you will see the way you can invest extra meaning in the particular spots that you place them. This is similar to the way that a tarot card spread assigns a specific meaning to each spot. When you start to define spaces in your grid, you are able to control the way that the energies are flowing together in a more minute fashion. This can have a telling effect and be very significant, so don't worry about assigning meaning to each space until after you have already made a few crystal grids.

While it is called a *crystal* grid, there is no reason that you can't bring in other objects. Some people like to bring in seashells and other naturally occurring objects. Others will use items that have a particular meaning to them like a wedding ring or even a stuffed toy animal. You can bring in anything you want, so long as you understand what the item means to you because the meaning will greatly affect the energies you are working with. Also, keep in mind that, while you want to select crystals which support your intention, your grid can benefit from adding some crystals that help to amplify the power of the other crystals around it. So you might choose an intention which isn't strongly connected to clear quartz, but choose clear quartz to be a part of the grid anyway as it will reinforce the others.

After you make your crystal grid, you will want to leave it be for a while. Consider it almost like cooking an elaborate dish. You need to get all the ingredients together first to cook the dish, but before it can be served, it needs to sit for a little while so that everything falls into place. The energies from the crystals aren't going to gel together immediately. They need to be given a chance to co-habitat the same space and to settle in. Once they have, there will be a concrete and solid energy that is palpable. So don't expect a crystal grid to immediately start producing power the moment you add the last crystal. You need to remember to be patient. The power is growing.

Taking Them to Bed

We've seen a couple of different crystals that help us to ward off nightmares. You might think that is the only benefit to taking crystals with you to bed, but if you believe that, then you are cutting yourself off from a lot of potential positive energy that could help improve your life. We spend between seven to nine hours in bed every single day. For many of us, it is the most enjoyable part of the day. But it is also the least productive, as it is hard to achieve much when we're off in Neverland. Yet we could be leveling up our sleep by using crystals.

As with making a crystal grid, you want to consider your intentions before picking a crystal to bring to bed. If you are dealing with a lot of anxiety, then you might want to bring a smoky quartz or another of the crystals which help to remove toxic negativity from your life. But if you aren't dealing with anxiety, and, instead, you want to attract romantic love, then the smoky quartz wouldn't be nearly as effective as a rose quartz. By choosing the intention, you can ensure that you are promoting the most effective use of your sleep and absorbing positive energies.

Just like how we benefit from carrying crystals with us, we benefit from being close to them at night when we sleep. You can place a crystal on your nightstand, or even create a crystal grid and place it on your nightstand (though please take your time to build up to this). But for the best effect, you should put the crystal underneath your pillow. The under-the-pillow approach is doubly beneficial if you choose a crystal that is linked to the crown chakra on the top of your head. That isn't to say you won't feel the effects of a crystal that is linked to the root or sacral chakra when it is placed under your pillow, just that it is more effective the closer you can keep the associated chakra.

Make Jewelry

It is undeniable that there are many people who think that healing crystals are silly. Whether this comes from a place of fear, envy, or ignorance, the reality is that it can be very annoying or even painful to have someone call you out for your beliefs. This is much more likely to happen if someone sees you creating a grid, meditating with a crystal, or the like. But the beauty of these crystals helps to show our belief loud and clear without drawing attention to it. Simply put, we can make jewelry out of our crystals. When you are wearing a necklace or a bracelet with a gorgeous crystal in it, you are more likely to have people ask you where you got it rather than insult your personal beliefs. Just wait to see the look on their face when you tell them that you made it yourself!

You don't have to make your own jewelry, of course. There are plenty of options available to get jewelry that integrates healing crystals. But when you make it yourself, there is a much stronger bond to both the crystals (as you chose the exact ones to include), as well as a sentimental value attached to it as a piece of jewelry. There are many guides online that aim to teach you how to make jewelry, and it is very easy to incorporate healing crystals into these tutorials. Plus, they are an absolute blast! There is such a sense of pride and joy that comes from making something yourself that you would be denying yourself a lot of happiness if you decided to skip out and just purchase a pre-made one. However, there is no shame at all in purchasing a piece of jewelry that has already been made. You still gain a wonderful piece of jewelry; it's just you don't get that feeling of pride that comes from the act of creation.

Healing crystal jewelry is also one of the best ways for us to get our crystals as close as possible to their corresponding chakra. We can create tiaras for our highest chakras, chokers for the neck, and necklaces to dangle down over our hearts. We can add healing crystals to a belt to get closer to the sacral and root. Or we can wear crystals in bracelets or anklets. This is a major plus that jewelry has over simply carrying our crystals with us.

Be careful about one thing when making your healing

crystal jewelry. I know it's been repeated to death, but you don't want to mix too many crystals until you are used to their energies. You might think it looks lovely to have five different crystals all on the same necklace, but then if the energy is overwhelming, you might find that wearing the necklace makes you feel like you are choking. When you first begin, start with jewelry that only has a single healing crystal. Next, you can add two more once you are used to them. You might want to try amplifying your original piece. Let's say you have a rose quartz necklace. Instead of adding more crystals to further the love energy, try adding a couple of clear quartz crystals that could amplify the strength of the original crystal. It is my suggestion that you first amplify your crystal before you alter the jewelry by adding other crystals to it.

Block Electromagnetic Fields

Everything that is alive produces an electromagnetic field. It is this field that gives us life, that allows us to think. There is a very surreal realization to be had when you start to look into electromagnetic fields, and you realize that we, as human beings, are continuously producing an electrical wave. We talk about "neurons firing" in our brains when we mean we are thinking about something or connecting ideas. It is almost crazy to realize that these thoughts, this firing, is an electric one. We are able to think because we create electromagnetic responses within ourselves.

But, it turns out, this also comes at a cost. Our modern society produces more electromagnetic fields than ever before. There are radio waves, cellular signals, and we are always looking at either a television, computer, or phone screen, and each of these devices produces an electromagnetic field. This is quite harmful to us. Consider the game of telephone that you played as a child. A message was whispered in one person's ear. That person would whisper to the next person, and it would go all around the classroom until it got back to the first person, at which point the message was so different as to be unrecognizable. The chaos of the game telephone is reflective of the chaos that happens to us when we're exposed to so many electromagnetic fields. Our thoughts have a harder time forming and coming together because there is so much interference between them due to outside forces.

There is still much research to be done regarding these fields, but many scientists believe they aren't healthy for us. Whether they contribute to the skyrocketing levels of anxiety in our modern society, or to physical poor health and illness, only time will tell. But enough has been explored on the topic to make even the bravest soul a little bit nervous once they start digging into it. Thankfully, some healing crystals are thought to have the ability to block out these electromagnetic fields and help us to remove ourselves from their onslaught. Malachite, black tourmaline, and shungite are just a few of the crystals which are considered to have this capability.

Blocking these fields is thankfully quite simple. Just purchase one of the crystals with these EMF blocking properties, and place them by any of the electronics in your house like your television or computer monitor. If people are right about these properties, then this is a way of protecting yourself from the harmful fields. If they are wrong, well, then you still have a beautiful looking crystal in your home as part of the decor. Plus, you can always use that crystal in a grid or add it to a piece of jewelry later on if you so choose.

Decoration

While you might think that this goes without saying, these crystals can make for wonderful decorations. They can add color to a room, and they can be used together or alone to create delightful highlights in any location in your house. While many people use crystals exactly for this reason, you shouldn't think that crystal decorations are simply pretty, and that's all. Remembering that these crystals have forceful energies, we need to be mindful of the way that they change the natural energy of the room. One of the reasons that crystals are often used for decoration is to promote a better sense of feng shui in a room, and this is certainly one amazing use, but to dig deep into feng shui would take a book all of its own.

Here we will content ourselves with speaking about general decorations.

Each room in your house has its vibration. A large part of this comes from the way that we invest personal energies into our living space. Using my quarters as an example, I have a kitchen, a bedroom, a living room, an office, and a bathroom. The bedroom has a relaxing energy, one that invites me to get a much deeper sleep than if I just laid down on the couch in the living room. The living room itself is relaxing, but there is a stronger sense of excitement and motion there, as I often entertain my guests there. In the kitchen, I have worked hard to create a sense of experimentation and play; it has a more random energy in which it feels like anything could happen at any moment. The office has a very focused and purposeful feeling, while the bathroom actually doesn't have much of an energy at all. These energies arise naturally from the way that I use and think about these rooms. I've also tried to promote my desired energy through the use of decorative crystals.

I have creative crystals in the kitchen, specifically tangerine quartz and Herkimer diamond. I have blue quartz and blue tiger's egg in the office. Amethyst and labradorite in the bedroom. Rose quartz, clear quartz, and amethyst round out the living room. I don't keep these crystals next to each other, as I prefer to spread them out to create almost a Venn diagram of energy in each room. But I have specifically chosen then for the vibrations that they promote. They look beautiful, and I have often received compliments on them, though my friends complimenting them didn't realize that I was using them for their energies. They simply saw a decoration that struck them as attractive. This is great, as there are several of my friends who would laugh if I told them the underlying purpose. Yet, I feel their comments are the clearest sign that it is working.

When deciding how to use crystals to decorate your home, start by considering what you want each room to promote. Happiness, love, lust, relaxation, creativity, all of these are valid choices, and they should be picked depending on your personal desires. Just because I like to have a relaxing energy in my bedroom doesn't mean you have to. You might be better suited by putting romantic or seductive crystals in your bedroom. It is entirely up to you, but you do need to figure out what you want ahead of time.

Once you know what you want to promote, it is time for the best part: setting up your decorative crystals. You may want to combine multiple crystals to form decorations, though you should have experience using multiple crystals at once before you do so. Or, you might do what I do and space them out to create a more even distribution of energy. Whatever you pick, simply keep your intentions in mind as you build or display your decorations. When you are mindful of the energy that the decorations are bringing, you are able to really, truly control the way that your home feels, and make it much more in line with your true self.

Chapter Summary

- Crystals make for powerful additions to a meditation session. You may want to hold your crystal, place it over one of your chakras, or stare at it as you meditate.

- Prior to meditating, figure out an intention that you want to bring into your life. This intention will help to pull energy from the crystal to infuse your life with its healing abilities.

- It is best to meditate twice a day to get the optimum effects.

- We can carry crystals with us throughout the day to benefit from their energy.

- When carrying crystals, it is best to keep them as close to ourselves as possible. Putting a crystal in a breast pocket is more effective than sticking it in your purse.

- Crystal elixirs are drinks that have been infused with the properties of a crystal. Be careful when making a crystal elixir, as some crystals are toxic, others dissolve in water, and yet others change form and become dangerous chemicals when introduced to water.

- You should always cleanse your crystals before using them as part of a crystal elixir.

- To make a crystal elixir, stick your chosen crystal into a bottle, cup, bowl, or pitcher of water and let it sit for a while. Then drink it when you are ready.

- You can use toxic crystals to make a crystal elixir, but they shouldn't be placed directly in the water. Instead, use a can or jar that has a lid and set the crystal on top of the lid. Let it stay that way overnight, as the lack of contact makes it take longer for the water to absorb the crystal's properties.

- Adding crystals to your bath can be an amazing method to create a more relaxing or meaningful experience. Be careful not to select crystals that are toxic. You could line the tub with them or have them nearby.

- You can combine a crystal bath with meditation for impressive results.

- A crystal grid is a pattern that you make with your crystals. The crystals work together to combine their energy and make a lasting effect. You need to leave a crystal grid to sit for several hours to let the vibrations properly align and mesh with each other.

- When making a crystal grid, let the crystals guide you to where they should be placed. Some people will tell you how they think a crystal grid should be done, but this is a personal opinion and not a set-in-stone rule.

- We often spend eight or more hours asleep every night. We can make productive use of this time by setting crystals on the nightstand or under our pillows so that their energies will infuse our lives while we sleep.

- Making jewelry is a great way to keep your crystals on you without drawing attention to your beliefs. Plus, there is a sense of pride that comes with creating something beautiful.

- Crystal jewelry is one of the easiest ways to keep our crystals close to the chakra that they are most associated with.

- Electromagnetic fields from devices are all around us, and they may well be harmful. Certain crystals are thought to help block out these fields to keep us safe. Simply place one of the blocking crystals next to your electronics.

- Crystals make for lovely decorations, but we should consider their placement carefully. We can set them out as decorations in such a fashion as to bring a positive or desired energy into the room.

- Crystals that are used as energy-inviting decorations should still be cleansed at least once a month.

In the next chapter, you will learn all sorts of tips that you can put to use to maximize your experience with your healing crystals. From techniques like combining crystals through to adding them into your daily routine, we'll cover everything you need to know in order to use your crystals like a pro.

CHAPTER FIVE

TIPS TO MAXIMIZE YOUR HEALING CRYSTALS

As we approach the end of the book, it might be helpful if we take a few minutes to consider some tips for maximizing the abilities and effectiveness of our healing crystals. We have briefly mentioned a few of these tips, and there is one that I hope you are already tired of hearing. But this chapter gathers these tips together to ensure that you leave with them fresh in your mind.

Even more than the tips we look at, you should pay special attention to the section on cleansing your crystals. If you are using them to remove negative energy from you, then nine times out of ten, this is going to be achieved by the crystal soaking up that negativity. If you don't cleanse the crystal, it will go bad and, instead of repelling negativity, it will invite that negativity. Obviously, this is the exact opposite of what we want, and so it is essential that you take this to heart and make sure you cleanse your crystals on a regular basis. You may choose to do this weekly, or you might fit the schedule to the phases of the moon. Pick the approach that is right for you. Speaking of right for you, that brings up to our first tip.

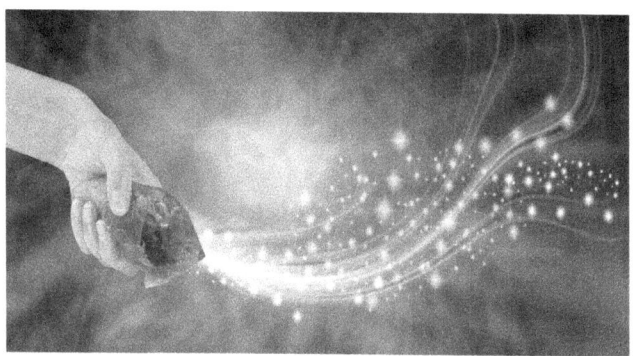

Let the Crystals Choose You

This particular tip is a little bit confusing because it contradicts other advice. Often when we go into the store or look to purchase crystals for the first time, we are best off going with one or two of the crystals that we looked at in chapter three. These have a more subtle energy that has a far smaller chance of swamping us. If we have never worked with energy before, these crystals are a great way to get started. But this isn't always the case. Sometimes, we are actually better advised to pick a strong crystal. The determining factor of which crystals are right for you isn't going to be anything that I have written here today, but rather it is going to be what you feel in your heart.

When you first look for crystals, you should try to open yourself up and be receptive to the vibrations that they are producing. This is best achieved in person. In fact, if you are only able to purchase your crystals online, then you should 100% stick to those listed in chapter three. But if you are able to purchase them in person, then try following these steps. Start by meditating before you go into the store. This doesn't need to be a long session, and, if need be, you can get away with taking a few deep breaths when you're on the sidewalk outside. The point of this is to take a moment to let your mind relax and open you up to the energy you are about to feel. More than anything else, this step is significant because the store you are about to enter is going to be bursting with energy, and you want to make sure that you are ready for that experience. When you aren't, you may find that the store spikes your anxiety or makes you feel deeply uncomfortable. Remember, this isn't the store itself, but the energies that are infused throughout it.

Next, once you have prepared yourself, enter into the store and navigate over to the crystals. You may have one or two that you intend to buy. Let yourself get these, but don't just go to the counter and rush off right away. Instead, take a few minutes to browse through the crystals available for purchase. You may want to reach your hand out and touch them or hover over them and be receptive to the way they make you feel. In all things to do with such energies, it is these feelings which should guide you first and foremost. If you feel compelled towards one of the crystals, then buy that one. It doesn't matter if it is the strongest crystal in that store. If your energy aligns with the crystal's energy, then you should go ahead and get it. Some of us are naturally drawn to certain powers. These energies might make another beginner sick, yet they fill you with a sense of purpose, calm, or connection.

Some people might argue that this could be dangerous. This is true; it can't be denied. It's possible for people to trick themselves into thinking they are more powerful than they are. Perhaps our vanity is providing unreliable advice. As part of your meditation beforehand, try to address your own sense of power and to approach the crystals the way that a newborn approaches the world. Try not to think of yourself as powerful. Instead, tell yourself that you have no power. This will help you to let go of your ego, which often tries to lead us down dangerous paths. Just keep in mind that this meditation is only for just before purchasing your crystal. After you get home, even before you use the crystals, take another moment to meditate for five or ten minutes. Instead of telling yourself anything, simply focus on your breathing and letting go of the earlier messages you told yourself. The truth is that you are powerful, even if that power isn't the kind necessary to use stronger crystals. Each of us has a power inside. We need to deny it and shut ourselves off from it if we want to open ourselves up to crystals for the first time, but to tell ourselves this throughout the day or, indeed, our life would be detrimental.

By letting the crystal choose you, you ensure that you are working with energies that flow naturally through you. That will reduce the amount of discomfort you feel when working with these healing crystals for the first time.

Keep in mind that you should also let the crystals pick the best approaches for their use. Sometimes we have specific uses for our crystals, such as meditation or decoration, but often we use the same crystals for several different purposes. You might carry a crystal in your pocket, use it as part of a grid later, and then create a crystal elixir with it at the end of the day. If you know that you want to work with a specific crystal, but you aren't sure to what end you should use it, consult the crystal. Hold it in your hand and see how it makes you feel. It will be able to suggest the most appropriate way of using it and benefiting from the vibrational powers it holds.

Start Slow, Add More in Time

It has been mentioned again and again, but it is so important that it deserves to have its own section in this chapter. When you first get your hands on your crystals, you are going to want to make all sorts of different spreads. If you are looking to benefit from their energies, there is a high chance you are going to use them in conjunction with one another. This is something that we do when working with healing crystals, but it is something that we need to build up to and embrace slowly.

When we try to use too many crystals at once, we become overwhelmed, and we can experience unhappy results. This happens when we severely mess up our own energy. The result is confusion, depression, anxiety, a sense of things not being right, but without a clear cause. It isn't until we sit and we meditate and properly realign our chakras that we realize it was our energy that was the problem. It is easy to think that perhaps we are stressed out due to work, love, family, money. But these are all external causes when the real cause was coming from inside of us.

In the last section, we saw that it can be okay sometimes to go with a strong crystal early. You absolutely should not be combing a strong crystal like this with another until you are quite experienced with your crystals. But even if you go with a more subtle crystal for beginners, you shouldn't be combing these together. That is a recipe for disaster you don't want to cook up.

It can be hard to be patient, especially when we live in a society with a 24/7 news cycle, online shopping, and instant messaging. But crystals aren't subject to modern fashions, and they shouldn't be rushed. Please, use these with caution and take your time. It is better to go too slow than to go too fast. Consider it like a car. If you crash going 10 miles an hour, then you are going to be okay. If you crash at 100 miles an hour, then you are much more likely to suffer injury or worse. When it comes to "driving" our crystals, we want to start slow before we ramp up the speed.

Cleanse Your Crystals Often and Thoroughly

As mentioned above, we need to cleanse our crystals to keep them working at their best. The first time that we cleanse our crystals should be as soon as we get them home from the store. Then we'll want to purify them regularly or after we use them, depending on what we are using them for. For example, crystals should be cleansed prior to being used to make a crystal elixir. Healing crystals worn as jewelry, carried throughout the day, or used as decoration should be cleansed at least once a month, though it is better to go for twice a month if you can.

The reason for this is these crystals often don't just create energy, they also absorb it. So if we want to keep a crystal positive, we need to get rid of the negativity that it has absorbed. You may choose to cleanse your crystals in certain ways. For example, you might group together red crystals to cleanse one way, but cleanse blue crystals another. Below are several different ways that you can cleanse your crystals, but there isn't one that is especially better than another. As with choosing your crystals, it is best to let the crystal inform the purifying ritual that is right for it. With that in mind, the first two cleansing rituals we'll look at are far and away the most popular.

For an easy way to cleanse your crystal, use natural water. It is important to avoid using water that has been processed or bottled. You may be able to use tap water, but if you have a nearby stream, lake, or pond, then this water will be much more effective. It would also be terrific if you have access to well water. But the best possible choice, if it is an option, is to use rain as it is coming down. We aren't always able to do this since we should be cleansing our crystals often, and sometimes the rain seems like it is never going to come. But if you see that it is raining, this can be a terrific time for an impromptu cleansing session. Simply take your crystal outside and let it sit in the rain for ten minutes. If you don't have the option of using rain, then use one of the other sources of water for ten to fifteen minutes. Keep in mind that the stronger the flow of water, the less fitting it is for use with brittle crystals that could be damaged. If you are looking to cleanse a fragile crystal, then you're better suited with this next approach.

Both sunlight and moonlight can be used to cleanse a crystal. Of the two, sunlight could potentially damage the crystal and cause it to lose or change color. The result of that could be detrimental to the crystal's power, so make sure that you research your crystal to see if it is safe for sunlight. If not, that's okay. As it turns out, moonlight is much more powerful than sunlight when it comes to cleansing. If you are going to use the light of the moon to cleanse your crystals, wait until the moon is full. A full moon is a source of great power, and its beams will help to clean out your crystals and keep them working to their full potency, without the risk of discoloration.

If you are looking to cleanse a crystal that is connected with the earth, then you can use earth itself as a way of cleansing it. Black tourmaline, citrine, malachite, rose quartz, smoky quartz, and rhodochrosite are just a few of the crystals that can be cleansed in this manner. To purify a crystal using earth, go out into the backyard and carefully bury them. The energy of the earth will detoxify the crystal, though you need to consider the timing of this particular ritual carefully. You will want to leave the crystals in the earth for at least 24 hours, though they will benefit from longer stretches. Bear in mind that means that you will be without those crystals and so you can't rely on their energy should you need it.

For those crystals that are connected to fire, such as fire

agate, aventurine, calcite, or garnet, you can purify them with fire. You need to be extremely careful when using fire for a cleansing ritual, as it can be easy to harm yourself if you aren't careful. You want the crystals to benefit from direct connection with the fire so that any negativity that has been trapped inside of them can be burnt away. While the smoke from the fire itself has some cleansing attributes, and your crystal will benefit from being exposed to it, you should take a pair of tongs or something and quickly stick the crystal into the flame. You only need to do this for five to ten seconds, as the cleansing properties of fire are quick to take effect and destroy the impurities.

Another fairly standard way of cleansing a crystal is to use saltwater. Salt has been used in magic rituals throughout history, and it has a very purging effect on negative energy. There is a reason why people would throw a handful of salt over their shoulders to ward off bad luck. Crystals should be left in a saltwater mixture overnight. Use sea salt rather than the kind you put on your french fries. If you have an ocean nearby, you can leave them in the water overnight for the best results. Just make sure that you use a bag or some other means of preventing them from being washed out to sea. As with rainwater, there are some crystals that don't benefit from this method as the salt can damage them. Plus, there are crystals that dissolve in water or change their structure, so always make sure you research the best method of cleansing any particular crystal before you embark on the ritual.

Be Willing to Experiment

Throughout this book, we have discussed many different crystals and many different ways of using them. I have recommended crystals that are suitable for beginners and have talked you through cleansing them. But none of this should be considered the end of the road when it comes to learning and experimenting with them. We are dealing with energy here, and the one thing that is a constant when it comes to energy is that the individual's relationship with that energy is unique and fertile. If you have reached this far in the book, you might think that you know everything you need to know about crystals. While you know everything you need to get started using them, no book, no matter how long it is, could fully cover the unique and malleable features of working with energy or crystals. To fully align with your crystals, you need to open yourself up and be ready to experiment.

We see this most clearly in our discussion of crystal grids. You can feel where each crystal needs to be placed, but what you feel is not going to be the same as what your best friend feels or what I feel. If we each had the same crystals, we would still walk away with a unique grid that reflects us personally. That is because nobody has the same energy as another person. So, instead of following everything that is written about crystals, you need to stay open. Try new things. Try combinations that you haven't seen people talk about. See if you can't figure out a new way to use your crystals, such as creating three-dimensional grids or infusing them directly into your work. Maybe you find that rolling a crystal is a more effective way of making a choice than rolling a dice. Perhaps you are an artist, and you find that using crystals to help you select colors or even to paint turns out to be beneficial. There are endless possibilities, so long as you are willing to experiment.

Chapter Summary

- Despite the fact that we should be cautious when we're a beginner, we shouldn't avoid powerful stones if they call to us.

- If you are buying your crystals online, stick to the ones for beginners as you won't be able to judge how the stronger ones make you feel.

- Before going into the store to purchase crystals, take a moment to meditate. A few deep breaths are all that is needed. You may want to tell yourself that you aren't powerful, so as to quiet down the ego.

- In the store, look at each of the crystals available and let yourself be drawn in naturally to any that call out to you.

- You should cleanse your crystals immediately after buying them.

- While you may want to jump into the deep end and make crystal grids with dozens of different types, you should start with a single crystal and then slowly work your way up from there.

- Being overwhelmed by the energy of your crystals can cause anxiety and feelings of not belonging. That could be the equivalent of blowing a fuse and it might really mess with your chakras.

- Crystals should be cleansed after they are purchased, before being used to make crystal elixirs, and at least once a month at the minimum.

- The easiest way to cleanse a crystal is to use natural water, such as leaving it outside in the rain for five to ten minutes.

- Sunlight can be used to cleanse a crystal, but light from the full moon is far more powerful and effective.

- Earth crystals can be buried in the ground for 24 hours as a way of cleansing.

- Fire crystals can be cleansed by being put in flame for five seconds.

- Saltwater will also work to purify crystals. Crystals should be placed in saltwater overnight; just make sure your crystals aren't the kind that are damaged by salt.

- While everything in this book has been to help you get started, you should be ready to toss it all out and go with your gut. Listen to your crystals.

- Be willing to experiment and try new things with your crystals.

FINAL WORDS

As the book comes to a close, we approach the end of our time together. It has been my hope that I was able to give you a better understanding of these powerful tools. While they are called healing crystals, it should be clear by now, this doesn't mean they replace medical care. These crystals can serve to help us heal physically, but they are most concerned with our emotional, mental, and spiritual well-being.

This is important; our emotional and spiritual health is highly threatened in our 21st-century culture. We are expected to work longer hours, to push ourselves to achieve more, and yet we are also supposed to keep up with the news and stay active on social media or be reachable by texts at all hours of the day. It's a way of life that creates a lot of pressure on us, demands that aren't normal for the human animal. We have developed over centuries to get to where we are, but we have forgotten how important it is to keep our spiritual and psychological health in check. We often come unaligned from our deepest self, and this causes us a lot of pain.

Healing crystals are one of the many ways we can use to help us to repair this damage. We saw in chapter one that these crystals are used for many different purposes, though almost all of them had one thing in common: they are used for healing some aspect of ourselves. It could be letting go of pain, learning to relax, warding off negative energy and inviting positivity, or accessing other elements of our potential.

It's vital not to ignore the emotional side of our existence, yet we so often do. We might be having issues relaxing, letting go of stress and anxiety, or even finding our happiness. Chapter two showed us how many different crystals can be used to achieve whatever emotional effect we are after. But not every crystal is suitable for beginners. That's why we looked at those crystals with a subtle energy in chapter three. If you are ordering your crystals online, then you should stick to those crystals we discussed in that chapter.

Crystals can be used as jewelry, as part of meditation, or even to infuse our water with their healing properties. Chapter four looked at the many ways that we might want to use crystals. Chapter five then looked at how we can maximize our experience with these crystals to have the most beneficial and positive time possible. One of the key points here was to open up and be willing to experiment. You shouldn't only rely on what we talked about in chapter four, but be adventurous in finding new ways of using your crystals.

Remember that no matter what you hear or what people say, the relationship that you have to your crystals will be the clearest way to define what is right and wrong. If you are drawn to a powerful crystal, it could be that you have an energy that matches it appropriately. Likewise, you should be willing to explore new ways of benefiting from your relationship with your crystals. If you approach them with this mindset, you will have a much easier and enjoyable experience working with them as they bring positive energy into your life.